BY ANY DREAMS NECESSARY

By Any Dreams Necessary

ANTI-RACIST STRATEGIES FOR SUSTAINABILITY, RESILIENCE AND ENVIRONMENTAL JUSTICE IN AFRICAN AMERICAN COMMUNITIES.

BRUCE W. STROUBLE JR.

Enlightened Learners Publishing

Published in Tallahassee, Florida, USA

Published by
Enlightened Learners Publishing
PO BOX 3581
Tallahassee, FL 32315
United States

For permissions, please contact:
info@brucestroublejr.com

Strouble, Bruce
By Any Dreams Necessary: Anti-Racist Strategies for Sustainability, Resilience, and Environmental Justice in African American Communities

ISBN: 979-8-218-46433-2
EISBN: 979-8-218-46434-9

Library of Congress Control Number: 2024918885

Cover Design by   Jewel Brown

Printed in the United States of America.

Dedication

I often wonder where I would be
if our ancestors hadn't dared to dream of being free.
I look to my children, hoping this work pays my debt forward,
Knowing that one day, my debt will be yours.
To my wife and mother, aunts, uncles, father, cousins, and
brothers,
keep your heads up—rise above it all—don't let the hate get
you flustered.
To those who suffered so that others could survive,
I dedicate this to you in hopes that our children will thrive.
You organized and protested, fought back and contested,
Only to be brutalized and despised, neglected and disrespected.
Through sundown towns, you came home to crosses burned on
your lawns. You may have passed, but look what your efforts
have spawned.
This is for the fallen and the unborn.
Consider these words a pledge we have sworn.
We will keep pushing forward, always remembering to look
back,
Persevering like Harriet and resisting like Nat.
Outlasting their systems, too smart for their traps—
defending your dreams—by any means - until it's safe to be
Black.

Contents

Preface

As I set out to write *By Any Dreams Necessary: Anti-Racist Strategies for Sustainability, Resilience, and Environmental Justice in African American Communities*, I found myself grappling with a relentless urge to confront the systemic challenges that continue to plague Black communities across America. This book emerged as my personal response to the overwhelming despair and hopelessness I often felt when faced with the totality of the existential crises facing all humanity, especially African People.

Growing up in the United States as a Black man, I witnessed first-hand the profound impact of systemic racism on families and entire communities. From a young age, I haphazardly observed loved ones cave under the pressure of virulent systemic oppression. Later, with heightened curiosity, I observed how internalized self-hatred tore apart families and weakened once close-knit communities, accelerating their social erosion amid the pressures of mass incarceration and gentrification. Media portrayals, from news outlets to Hollywood films, perpetuated a narrative of self-victimization without providing a complete context. These experiences led me to internalize doubts about the capabilities of Black people. I often found myself questioning: "Is there something wrong with us? Why do we have so many problems? Why can't we get it together?"

Fortunately, my parents, both attendees of the prestigious Historically Black Howard University, exposed me to anti-racist philosophy and African-centered thought, which shielded me from the ever-present pervasive anti-black propaganda. The seeds they planted were nourished by hip-hop music that encouraged Black pride and perseverance. I immersed myself in the teachings of Malcolm X, Harriet Tubman, Nat Turner, Patrice Lumumba, Amos Wilson, and Nelson Mandela while listening to KRS-One, Public Enemy, X Clan, Nas, Ice Cube, The Roots, Tupac, and Ras Kass. However, it wasn't until I began my studies at the Historically Black Florida A&M University that I was fully awakened to the gravity of African people's historical and ongoing challenges. The harsh reality was that Africans were forcibly taken from their homeland, dispersed across the diaspora, and exploited to enrich others, diminishing their capacity to address their collective issues. Further, the legacy of traumatic events left a legacy of cumulative residual impacts on our contemporary physical and mental health as well as our economic and political well-being. I realized that without feasible solutions, these problems would fester into a collective depression, stifling creativity and perpetuating the dysfunction within our families and communities.

In conversations with colleagues, friends, and family, we often discuss many of the challenges and potential solutions. Those conversations often left us with uneasy feelings of uncertainty and dread. I suspect that following the 2024 elections, similar feelings have gripped most of us who have been burdened with the desire for progress. My remedy to mitigate those deleterious feelings and avoid the resulting depression and apathy has been to throw myself into action. Early in my career, when I first discovered this internal strife, I immersed myself in learning about Black history and responses to oppression. I joined multiple organizations and collaborated with some of our time's most influential advocates and activists. I dedicated my professional life to studying and addressing our people's problems. To keep it 100, this was not solely for altruistic reasons but also to cajole myself to carry on in otherwise overwhelming circumstances.

At its core, *By Any Dreams Necessary* is my best effort at developing a blueprint for sustainable development and enhanced resiliency within Black communities based on what I have learned in my academic and professional work. It synthesizes insights from Social Capital Theory and Critical Race Theory and uses the Polarities of Democracy framework to propose a holistic approach to community empowerment. Through rigorous research, community-based insights, and strategic recommendations, this book is intended to empower Black communities to survive and thrive through and beyond hostile circumstances.

I hope *By Any Dreams Necessary* catalyzes dialogue and action. I want this work to inspire policymakers, community leaders, activists, and educators to dream big as they pursue justice, equity, and resilience. Our outlook may be gloomy, but I sincerely believe the audacity to dream of a better future is the first step in creating that future. A future where African people live in sustainable, thriving communities is one of my many dreams, and this work is my effort to transform this dream into reality.

In solidarity and determination,

Dr. Bruce W. Strouble Jr.

1

Dreaming of a Black Future

*"I'd give a dim-lit dream a color scheme" –
Cee Lo Green.*

Setting the Stage for Change

Growing up Black in the United States of America has always demanded the suppression of my raw and honest emotional expressions. As Black Americans, we often find our true feelings anchored in a sea of racial animus. From a young age, Black boys learn that the repercussions of our actions or emotional outbursts will likely result in adverse outcomes. Many Black families have histories of trauma surrounding Black men and women who spoke out against injustice only to be vilified and destroyed. We have all seen what has become of those seekers of justice who came before us. They were beaten, lynched, socially ostracized, economically neutralized, and used to teach a haunting lesson to all who would follow in their footsteps. These lessons remain entrenched in the Black collective memory and are routinely amplified by the ceaseless cadence of cautionary narratives from those who surrendered to the oppression. "Don't let them white folks hear you talking like that," they whisper. "Nothing we can do about that." "Better them than us." "That's just the way it is," they murmur as if to rationalize the ceaseless injustice that flows around and through Black bodies from the moment their first breath is taken.

Unpacking the Black Experience

The psychological toll of living with constant racial animus is immense. Racism in America is not relegated to isolated incidents that occasionally haunt our existence; it is the very prism through which our daily experiences are refracted. It is a constant, uninvited companion in the journey of the Black experience. Acknowledging this reality is daunting, yet ignorance exacts a more deleterious toll. Left unchecked, this hostile racial reality indoctrinates many Black people to view disparity as standard and normative. The message sent to our youth resounds with a staggering clarity: "Your life does not matter." "You are not important." "Stay in your place and be satisfied with day-to-day survival." This perspective, when adopted by a critical mass of Black people, is unequivocally unsustainable. It nurtures dysfunctional communities that stifle our collective mental health and socio-economic development.

The Spirit of Black Resistance

Despite the varying challenges facing Black communities, the beauty and resilience of the Black people persist. Seemingly, through the struggles of our ancestors, a contingent of us remain resolutely poised to forge ahead against all odds in pursuit of justice, liberation, and freedom for our people. The enduring spirit of resistance flows through our sermons, poetry, rap lyrics, artworks, lectures, and literature—beacons passed from generation to generation, symbolizing hope and determination. It is within the embrace of this spirit that I am drawn to confront the contemporary challenges that confront Black Americans today.

Contemporary Struggles

This very moment, Black children are being inundated with toxic poisons that are legally sited near their schools and homes, hospitalized from asthma, cancer, and lead exposure, sex trafficked, abused, murdered, undereducated, and incarcerated at alarmingly disproportionate rates when compared to their counterparts in other racial groups. Yet, despite our nation's technological advancement and economic superiority, little is being done to address these issues. The leaders in the Democratic party repeatedly fail to adequately prioritize these issues, while the Republican Party actively seeks to worsen conditions for Black people. These circumstances created the urgency with which I started trying to answer some critical questions. How do we survive in a system seemingly designed against us? How can we plan for the future when our history underscores the uncertainty of our present? And perhaps the starkest question: what happens to the next generations of Black people if we fail to answer these questions successfully?

All things considered, the United States stands as one of the world's most enduring and influential perpetrators of White Supremacist ideology. While some might argue that Nazi Germany represented the most extreme manifestation of White Supremacy, the U.S. has pioneered a modernized and insidious style of this ideology. This evolution was not born out of moral reckoning but instead forced by the strength of progressives committed to advancing a more democratic society. Without their persistent resistance, the U.S. might well have resembled other ethno-states, defined by rigid racial hierarchies and unchecked oppression.

The progress was more of a negotiation than a transformation, a tenuous, informal treaty between White and Black Americans. This "agreement" pacified many Black communities, offering incremental improvements without addressing core systemic inequities while leaving White extremists deeply dissatisfied. Beginning in the late 1950s, the U.S. embarked on a path of micro-measures to improve race relations, presenting the illusion of progress while maintaining the structure of systemic oppression.

As of 2025, however, the fragile gains of this uneasy treaty are rapidly unraveling. Right-wing extremists and conservative forces have accelerated efforts to erode these hard-won advancements, aiming to restore more traditional manifestations of patriarchal White Supremacy. What was once a slow unraveling has become a dismantling, threatening the already tenuous peace and reigniting the need for bold, unyielding resistance.

In recent years, we've witnessed a troubling resurgence of proto-fascist and anti-Black ideologies within the mainstream. These old-fashioned racist ideologies threaten to unravel the minuscule progress and hard-fought gains that Black people have achieved through generations of human rights struggles. As a Black man, my deepest fear is that we are witnessing the gradual erosion of these gains, further decreasing the chances of Black people surviving and sustaining within an unsustainable system.

The looming climate crisis is an existential threat that compounds all other dangers facing humanity, with Black Americans bearing a disproportionate burden. This crisis is intrinsically linked to the increasing and unsustainable consumption of greenhouse gas-emitting fossil fuels. The irony is palpable: rising temperatures, sea levels, and unpredictable weather patterns—expected to incur trillions in damages and claim millions of lives over the next few decades—are the direct result of colonial practices that enslaved Africans and displaced Indigenous Americans to generate wealth for White men. European colonialism not only exploited human lives but also set the stage for the environmental degradation we face today, leaving marginalized communities across the "Global South" to suffer the most from its consequences.

As our country remains politically gridlocked, seemingly accelerating toward its self-induced demise, these colossal challenges create the illusion that Black issues are separate and secondary, relegating them to the periphery of urgent discussions. Anti-woke campaigns attempt to whitewash America's bloody history, and climate change deniers continue to sanction toxic pollution, confining Black Americans to the lower decks of a sinking ship that is the USA. It is imperative that Black communities prepare lifeboats and escape plans and say prayers as we brace for the worst while hoping for the best.

The reality is that many of our liberal and progressive White allies, for various reasons, have shown themselves either unable or unwilling to provide the protection and support that we need. We find ourselves in a precarious position, lacking any tools for self-determination that exist outside the framework set by our oppressors. There's a conspicuous absence of collective plans or platforms to drive sustainable changes that we widely support, even within our communities. At most, we react to extreme cases of police brutality or unfavorable policy with protests, calls for unorganized voting, and social media hashtags, a timid response to a deeply entrenched problem.

It becomes increasingly evident that we need strategists and planners to chart a course through these challenging times. We require a roadmap that not only safeguards our gains but also paves the way for a more just and sustainable future for Black Americans.

Framing the Discussion

The journey began with a desire to understand the keys to establishing sustainable African American communities. This quest steered me towards an in-depth exploration of social capital, a concept I believed was pivotal in this context. Upon examining the intricacies of social capital within African American neighborhoods, I uncovered its significant influence on our community's resilience. Furthermore, I recognized how the absence of social capital often underpins our persistent challenges. To effectively tackle these issues, I synthesized a strategic approach that combines the principles of the Empowerment Framework, the analytical lens of Critical Race Theory, and the governance insights from the Polarities of Democracy. This integrated approach is crafted to steer African American communities toward sustainability and resiliency.

Defining Key Terms

Before delving into proposed solutions, defining critical terms used throughout this work is crucial. These definitions ensure a shared understanding of the concepts discussed:

- African Americans: Refers to U.S. citizens of recent African descent (post-1500 A.C.E) who identify as Black or African American on the U.S. Census. It's used interchangeably with "Blacks."
- African American or Black community: These terms refer to groups of African American/Black people residing in census tracts where the Black population is the majority and at least 40% of all residents.

- ○ The term Low Diversity Majority Black Community (LDMBC) describes census tracts that are overwhelmingly populated by Black people (75% or more)
- Racism: Denotes the procedures, ideologies, and practices perpetuating racial inequality and affording privilege to the dominant racial group based on phenotypical characteristics.
- Anti-Racist: The intentional and active process of identifying, challenging, and opposing racism and its various forms and manifestations.
- Social Capital: The resources, benefits, and networks created and shared by members of social groups through social cohesion, trust, and civic engagement. It facilitates coordinated action to solve individual and collective problems.
- Sustainability: Refers to the concept of fulfilling the needs of current generations without compromising the needs of future generations while ensuring a balance between economic growth, environmental care, and social well-being.
- Resilience: A community's capacity to persist and maintain its level of functioning amid disturbances and its ability to adapt and transform in ways that enhance its functioning through future disturbances.
- Environmental Justice: The equitable treatment and meaningful participation of all people, regardless of race, color, national origin, or income, in the development, implementation, and enforcement of environmental laws, regulations, and policies, ensuring that no group experiences a disproportionate share of negative environmental consequences.

Acknowledgment of Potential Bias

As a Black scholar and activist, I must acknowledge my potential biases and the limitations of my research scope while striving for objectivity and amplifying the voices of the Black communities involved in the study. Recognizing that no single solution fits all, this book aims to offer a guiding framework adaptable to the unique needs of each Black community. I do not claim this work exhausts all ideas and approaches.

Book Overview

The following chapters are carefully arranged to provide a comprehensive journey through the complexities and aspirations of building a sustainable future for Black communities:

Chapter 2: Planning for the Future of Black America—Assessing Historical and Contemporary Plans and Platforms—The foundation is laid by reviewing historical and contemporary plans and initiatives for African Americans and critically analyzing their relevance and impact.

Chapter 3: Anatomy of a Black Community: Understanding Social Capital, Resilience, and Sustainability - Delving deeper into the heart of community development, this chapter explores the concepts of social capital and its pivotal role in fostering resilience and sustainability within Black communities. Drawing from academic research, it uncovers how social capital can be harnessed to empower these communities.

Chapter 4: Black in "AmeriKKKa": Racial Oppression and Its Impact on Black Communities—Building on the understanding of Black social capital, this chapter unveils the systemic nature of racism and its profound effects on social capital formation and access within Black communities. It explores the multidimensional impact of structural and internalized racism.

Chapter 5: The State of Black America—This chapter comprehensively examines the demographic trends shaping the African American experience, focusing on relevant data from 2000 to 2020.

Chapter 6: Assessing Strengths, Weaknesses, Opportunities, and Threats in Black America—This chapter analyzes Black communities' unique strengths and weaknesses to identify internal and external factors influencing community development and resilience. The goal is to leverage strengths, address weaknesses, seize opportunities, and mitigate threats.

Chapter 7: Strategic Priorities for Black Empowerment and Progress—Building upon the insights from the SWOT analysis, this chapter presents a wide range of strategies for advancing sustainability, resilience, and environmental justice within Black communities.

Chapter 8: Power to the People: Leveraging Democracy to Advance Anti-Racist Policies—This chapter will translate the insights from the SWOT analysis into tangible goals, strategic actions, and policy recommendations. Collectively, these elements serve as a roadmap for Black communities, offering guidance and actionable steps for community organizations and governments.

Chapter 9: Implementing the Vision: Interventions for Black America's Sustainable Future - This chapter focuses on actionable steps and strategic interventions. It presents adaptable models derived from research and experience to kickstart the creation of sustainable and resilient African American communities.

Chapter 10: From Dreams to Reality: Forging a Sustainable Future for Black Communities—In the final chapter, I issue a call to action, urging readers, policymakers, and community leaders to actively engage in dismantling oppressive structures and advocating for equitable access to resources, education, and economic opportunities. This chapter emphasizes the need to challenge the status quo and collectively unite to pursue better, sustainable, resilient communities.

A Collaborative Journey Informed by Lived Experiences

This work is a call to action for progress and a brighter future, inviting you to participate in a transformative strategic process. Our mission is clear: we must be intentional about the survival of Black people on this planet. This requires that we build resilient, sustainable communities where our people can thrive. Our efforts can involve various partnerships but must not rely on permission or support from non-Black people.

Overcoming racism and white supremacy is an arduous challenge for African Americans that demands an unprecedented collaborative effort. To accomplish the feat in the shadow of a worsening climate crisis further exacerbates the urgency. I take no shame in admitting I do not have all the answers. However, I am confident that research-driven, strategic approaches focusing on sustainability, resilience, and environmental justice increase the chances that we significantly enhance Black people's quality of life, economic opportunities, and political maturity.

Conclusion

This work aims to spearhead an effort that develops a vision and plan for the sustainable future of Black America. However, systemic racism imposes a web of interwoven obstacles that require advanced problem-solving to generate feasible solutions. My strategic planning and community organizing background has sharpened my skills in approaching complex issues. To this end, I examine the strengths, weaknesses, opportunities, and threats facing contemporary African American communities in the United States. I also review proposed solutions from activist groups, community organizers, academics, and politicians. By critiquing and evaluating these strategies, I aim to extract the best elements while addressing any identified flaws.

This research offers insights for community leaders and policymakers on the development and sustainability of Black communities and identifies barriers that must be surmounted. It also sets the stage for future research on racism's impact, which could lead to better mitigation strategies.

Therefore, I urge readers, especially policymakers and community leaders, to draw inspiration from our forebears and see beyond the current status quo. We must engage beyond academic and activist circles and act within our communities. Change requires our direct involvement, policy reform, and collective effort. We recognize that change is not abstract; it requires active engagement, policy reform, and collective action. However, we are not simply spectators in the political landscape but active participants, architects of our own destiny.

In the following pages, we will unravel a story woven with resilience, transformation, and hope. It is a story that underscores the power of social capital and community and its essential role in fostering sustainable, resilient Black communities. This is more than an academic exploration; it is a plea for ongoing action towards a better future—a future where Black youth are unburdened by systemic racism and their aspirations are achievable. Together, we can build that future where Black lives truly matter. But, to accomplish such an audacious task, we must be willing to break free from the entrapments of our day-to-day survival routines and cultivate the seeds of our sustainable future By Any Dreams Necessary!

2

Planning for the Future of Black America

Planning for Black America's Future

In the quest for justice, equality, and empowerment, the landscape of political advocacy and policy-making for African American communities in the United States is marked by a rich history of diverse strategies and proposals. These efforts aim to tackle the multifaceted challenges faced by Black Americans and leverage their considerable potential for growth and advancement. However, amidst the many proposals, there is an apparent disparity between promises and tangible progress achieved. The question remains: which plans have resulted in genuine progress toward stated goals, and how can these efforts be evaluated, enhanced, and reutilized for future success?

In this chapter, we undertake a critical examination and comparative analysis of several influential contemporary plans and policy agendas that profess to serve the interests of African Americans. While not exhaustive, this selection will offer insights into these initiatives' shared objectives and methods, providing a foundational understanding of the prevailing approaches to empowerment and advocacy. The selected plans reflect those I could locate using a Google search. I then reviewed the plans for minimum qualifications of a national agenda for African American people's advancement. Aside from these prerequisites, I discarded plans that did not have what I determined to be remotely feasible action items based on contemporary political, economic, and social settings.

The Anatomy of a Good Plan

At the core of a successful plan for Black Americans is clarity of purpose. It should have a well-defined objective that directly tackles the challenges it seeks to overcome. Ambiguity can lead to confusion and hinder progress. Therefore, a clear focus is vital.

Comprehensive analysis is another cornerstone. A plan must be grounded in an objective and thorough examination of the problems it aims to solve. This analysis should consider the historical context, current conditions, and future trends, ensuring it addresses the root causes of issues. We accomplish this by conducting a Strengths, Weaknesses, Opportunities, and Threats (SWOT) Analysis and Situational assessment of the state of Black Americans.

Specificity is key. Rather than offering vague recommendations, a good plan outlines concrete steps, timelines, and responsibilities. It leaves no room for ambiguity, making implementation smoother. Measurable goals and benchmarks are necessary. A plan should establish clear criteria for success and regularly evaluate progress to determine if it is achieving its intended outcomes. Also, while the plan may include measures that would make general improvements, it is exceptionally critical to have elements strategically aligned with the collective needs of Black American Communities.

Engagement and inclusivity are essential. To be effective, a plan should involve input and perspectives from the communities it aims to serve. Stakeholders at all levels, including community members, experts, and policymakers, should be engaged to ensure diverse voices and experiences are reflected. Furthermore, equity and inclusivity should be guiding principles, ensuring that the plan addresses systemic disparities and promotes inclusivity, not perpetuating existing inequalities.

Resource allocation cannot be overlooked. Adequate funding, personnel, and technology must be allocated to implement the plan effectively. Without these resources, even the most well-conceived plan can falter. Yet, flexibility is crucial because circumstances change over time. A plan should be adaptable and responsive to unforeseen challenges and opportunities.

Common Planning Pitfalls

Common planning pitfalls across these initiatives include a lack of specificity in terms of funding, legislation, and implementation. Furthermore, political opposition has been a recurring challenge, often stemming from divergent ideological perspectives on these critical issues. Additionally, securing the necessary financial resources and addressing budget constraints can be formidable hurdles, especially in a climate where budget priorities and deficit concerns are prominent. Finally, fostering community engagement and ensuring the sustainability of these plans beyond a single presidential term are issues that require careful consideration.

Understanding these pitfalls provides valuable insights for future iterations of plans aimed at addressing racial disparities. Specificity in policy proposals, including legislative details and funding mechanisms, is critical for effective planning. Acknowledging potential political opposition and actively seeking bipartisan support can increase the likelihood of successful implementation. Addressing budget constraints through innovative financing and resource allocation strategies is essential for turning plans into action. Lastly, actively involving affected communities in the planning process and ensuring a mechanism for long-term sustainability can enhance the impact of these initiatives. By learning from past experiences and avoiding these common pitfalls, future racial justice and equity plans can be better equipped to effect lasting change.

Reviewing Historic and Contemporary Plans

To effectively evaluate each plan, we will apply a structured assessment that considers the historical and social context, evaluates the strengths, identifies challenges, and gauges overall feasibility. The latter part of the chapter will then draw comparative insights to distill common themes and inform the development of a comprehensive, forward-looking strategy.

The Black Panther Party for Self-Defense - 10 Point Platform, 1966

Originating in the 1960s during the Civil Rights Movement, the Black Panther Party for Self-Defense, commonly known as the Black

Panthers, emerged as a radical force advocating for the rights and well-being of Black Americans. Their 10-Point Platform was a manifesto addressing systemic racism, discrimination, and economic exploitation. Its demands were clear-cut, calling for an end to police brutality, equitable housing and employment, exemption from military service, and the release of Black individuals from incarceration for unjust reasons.

Strengths: The Black Panthers effectively amplified issues of systemic racism and inequality, shifting them from peripheral concerns to the forefront of national discourse. Their platform was a potent symbol of empowerment, inspiring Black individuals to assert their rights and combat oppression. Their comprehensive agenda recognized that the fight for equality spanned multiple domains, including economics, education, and the justice system. More importantly, the plan laid out specific goals that, if accomplished, would tremendously restructure African American communities, improving the quality of life for future generations.

Challenges: The platform's ambitious demands were not accompanied by detailed economic strategies or funding mechanisms, which cast doubt on their feasibility. The lack of a counter strategy to anticipated political opposition limited the platform's effectiveness. Also, the specific issues faced by Black women and other marginalized groups within the Black community were not adequately addressed with specificity. Furthermore, the plan failed to identify the internal problems at play within the community that were reinforcing external oppression. Lastly, the long-term sustainability of the proposed community programs lacked a clear operational blueprint. Examining the 10-point platform program suggests that the responsibility to resolve issues in Black communities rests on support from local, state, and federal agencies. With hindsight from a less hostile contemporary racial climate, the Panthers' 10 Point Platform has many shortcomings that, if addressed, could transform many of the aspirations into tangible community objectives.

Feasibility: Despite the Black Panthers' significant role in raising awareness, the implementation of their platform was impeded by governmental resistance, notably from the FBI, and by the controversial nature of their self-defense stance. While their legacy remains influential, many of their core objectives remain unfulfilled, underscoring the ongoing struggle against entrenched systemic inequalities.

Blueprint for Black Power: A Moral, Political, and Economic Imperative for the Twenty-First Century - Amos Wilson -1998

"Blueprint for Black Power," authored by Amos Wilson, presents a thorough strategy for African American self-empowerment against a backdrop of systemic discrimination. Central to Wilson's thesis is economic empowerment, political activism, educational advancement, psychological emancipation, and cultural preservation. Wilson's vision is one of unity and collective action; he sees community solidarity as a powerful tool to overcome social and economic challenges. The establishment of dedicated economic and political organizations is presented as a strategy for advocating Black interests and driving community development and self-sufficiency. Through these interrelated themes, "Blueprint for Black Power" serves as a strategic guide for achieving self-determination and lasting power for the Black community.

Strengths: Wilson's blueprint is comprehensive, addressing economic, political, psychological, and cultural facets of empowerment. The focus on economic independence and education is presented as pivotal to community empowerment. The alignment of objectives and prescribed actions is exceptionally detailed and well-organized.

Challenges: Wilson's blueprint requires more detailed collective economics and political engagement strategies. Overcoming entrenched disparities and systemic opposition is a complex challenge that requires targeted legal and political action. Initiatives for mental health and cultural preservation need to be more clearly articulated and resourced.

Feasibility: Wilson's vision, as expressed in *The Blueprint for Black Power,* confronts economic challenges, political resistance, and the erosion of cultural identity. The practical realization of Wilson's proposed strategies will require a sustained effort and a unified community response to dismantle the structural barriers and fulfill the promise of empowerment. This blueprint has exceptional utility and is foundational to developing African American empowerment plans.

PowerNomics: The National Plan to Empower Black America by Dr. Claud Anderson, 2001

PowerNomics: The National Plan to Empower Black America, by Dr. Claud Anderson, offers an integrated approach to combatting the economic and social inequities faced by Black Americans. Published in 2001, the book advocates for economic self-reliance as the linchpin for advancement. Central to the strategy are principles of land acquisition, establishment of economic enclaves, focused education, and collective community efforts aimed at wealth and resource control. Dr. Anderson emphasizes the critical role of group economics, encouraging Black Americans to leverage unity and shared purpose in building sustainable economic structures and pressing for systemic reform.

Strengths: "PowerNomics" is a visionary blueprint that champions economic empowerment as the key to addressing racial disparities. Dr. Anderson's approach is comprehensive, interweaving land acquisition, business development, and educational reform into a strategic plan aimed at economic self-reliance for Black Americans. The emphasis on ownership and community-centric business ecosystems seeks to cultivate a base for wealth generation that can endure over generations. This collective economics framework is not just about uplifting individuals; it is about revitalizing communities from within.

Challenges: Despite its merits, "PowerNomics" seemingly underestimates systemic barriers to resource acquisition and the complexities of changing institutional biases. The strategy's focus on self-sufficiency might also inadvertently reduce engagement with broader societal resources and economic systems that are critical to overcoming racial inequities. Furthermore, the changing global financial landscape calls for agile adaptations beyond traditional ownership and business models, which the plan may need to integrate.

Feasibility: Dr. Anderson's ambitious economic strategies confront significant hurdles: the uneven distribution of resources across Black communities and potential resistance from entrenched power structures that benefit from the status quo. While these strategies are practical, rallying a unified effort across the diverse spectrum of Black America presents additional challenges. Furthermore, some might argue that the plan is overly reliant on "Black Capitalism" and does not demonstrate adequate class consciousness necessary to reconcile economic disparities within Black communities. To improve the feasibility, the strategy must consider these complexities and foster unity and strategic alliances across communities.

The Contract for Black America - O'Shea "Ice Cube" Jackson (2020)

"The Contract for Black America," introduced by O'Shea "Ice Cube" Jackson in 2020 amid a surge in the movement for racial justice, is a broad proposal tackling systemic inequalities faced by Black Americans. It addresses key areas: criminal justice, economic opportunity, reparations, voting rights, and political representation. The contract calls for profound reforms in policing and the justice system, proposes reparations to compensate for historical injustices, and advocates for financial mechanisms to support Black businesses and reduce wealth disparities. Furthermore, it underscores the need to safeguard voting rights, fight voter suppression, and enhance political participation and representation for Black Americans.

Strengths: Ice Cube's *Contract for Black America* tackles systemic inequalities with various policy proposals. It boldly addresses reparations and economic justice, committing to rectifying historical wrongs. The plan's emphasis on political empowerment through voting rights and representation is crucial to effecting change within the democratic framework. Various proposals in the plan, such as "Baby Bonds," "Neo Reconstruction," and "Bank Lending Reforms," are cleverly designed to have far-reaching impacts, advancing African American communities.

Challenges: "The Contract for Black America" assumes a level of governmental cooperation that may be overly optimistic. It presents innovative economic strategies but does not fully address the current biases in financial systems or the deep-rooted issues affecting financial literacy. Furthermore, "The Contract for Black America" lacks a critical class analysis and instead purports capitalist solutions that would likely continue class-based issues within the African American community. Additionally, the path to reparations and heightened political representation is fraught with potential for resistance and complexity, suggesting a need for more nuanced strategies to realize these objectives.

Feasibility: Implementing the sweeping reforms of "The Contract for Black America" may be challenging due to the pushback from political and economic institutions resistant to change. The requirement for significant investments and a cooperative political environment presents additional layers of complexity to the plan's actionable trajectory. Successful implementation will hinge on overcoming systemic inertia and cultivating a consensus among a politically diverse populace.

The Congressional Black Caucus's Black American Agenda for the 118th Congress, 2023

Since its founding in 1971, the Congressional Black Caucus (CBC) has been at the forefront of advocating for Black Americans in Congress, targeting racial disparities across various sectors. In the 118th Congress, the CBC's comprehensive agenda includes bolstering democracy and civic engagement, supporting education through HBCUs and teaching Black history, pushing for environmental justice, and advancing clean energy. They aim to reduce health inequities, improve access to healthcare, address housing affordability and discrimination, and reform public safety with an emphasis on police accountability and community-driven solutions.

Strengths: The CBC's agenda showcases its holistic and insightful approach to tackling systemic issues, demonstrating how interrelated aspects of society affect Black Americans. By advocating for equitable voting rights, the Caucus ensures that African American representation and voices are preserved. Their educational policies emphasize empowerment through knowledge, supporting institutions critical to developing Black leaders, and advocating for historical accuracy in academic content.

Their focus on environmental justice ties directly to health outcomes and economic progress, emphasizing sustainable development. Health initiatives are dedicated to providing comprehensive healthcare access and addressing specific health conditions prevalent within Black communities. Housing policies aim to ensure equitable access to safe and affordable housing, combating discrimination and its consequences.

Challenges: Despite these strengths, the CBC's agenda faces challenges in transforming these ambitious goals into tangible legislation. More detailed legislative language and actionable steps are needed to move from vision to reality. A transparent budgetary framework and bipartisan support are crucial for funding and implementing these expansive initiatives. The CBC must also proactively engage with diverse political views to garner the necessary support for advancing its agenda. Additionally, incorporating measurable objectives and an evaluation framework is critical for tracking progress and accountability.

Feasibility: Partisan divisions, fiscal constraints, legislative complexities, and bureaucratic challenges pose significant barriers to the CBC's agenda. Moreover, the need for adaptability in a dynamic political environment is critical for maintaining progress toward achieving the Caucus's long-term objectives.

The Platinum Plan - President Donald Trump

The Platinum Plan, unveiled during President Donald Trump's 2020 re-election bid, aimed to uplift Black Americans by proposing initiatives across the economic, educational, criminal justice, and health sectors. The plan aimed to facilitate access to capital for Black businesses, expand Opportunity Zones, and create jobs, primarily via support for Historically Black Colleges and Universities (HBCUs) and school choice.

Strengths: Despite the many politicized critiques, President Trump's plan offered more ethno-specific objectives for African Americans than in previous administrations. Criminal justice reforms were to extend the First Step Act's initiatives, focusing on policing and community safety. Healthcare disparities were to be tackled through improved services and access, while economic measures included tax cuts, expansion of Opportunity Zones, home ownership, and financial literacy to address wealth inequality. The plan's proposal to create three million new jobs for the Black community was ambitious and, if realized, could have substantially lowered the Black unemployment rate, historically higher than the national average. Ultimately, the plan's breadth, covering a range of issues from economic support to healthcare and criminal justice reform, indicated a holistic vision to address the multifaceted challenges faced by Black communities.

Challenges: The Platinum Plan faced scrutiny over its timing, the administration's legacy, and lack of detail in implementation strategies. Critics pointed to its educational and criminal justice proposals as potentially ineffective or insincere. The absence of environmental justice considerations and techniques to tackle systemic racism was also a glaring omission. Additionally, the plan appeared to lack meaningful engagement with Black community leaders and organizations during its development, leading to questions about its legitimacy and whether it truly reflected the needs and aspirations of the community it purported to serve.

Feasibility: The Platinum Plan would likely face significant political and social barriers. Skepticism regarding Trump's political will, his administration's controversial legacy, and the timing of the plan's release all fed into doubts about its viability. Achieving legislative change would also be complex due to the polarized political environment and the necessity of support from the extreme anti-Black elements of Trump's power base, further complicating the plan's prospects for success. Although Trump wielded considerable influence within his party, the contentious nature of his leadership often requires that his political capital be expended on defending or navigating crises rather than on policy implementation. This results in less attention and fewer resources devoted to enacting new initiatives.

Lift Every Voice Plan for Black America - President Joe Biden - 2020

Joe Biden's equity advancement plan for African Americans aims to bridge economic disparities through enhanced support for Black businesses and workers, including funding and relief efforts. Educational initiatives seek to provide universal preschool, make college more affordable, and reduce student debt. The plan focuses on access and quality to address health disparities in healthcare. Criminal justice reform includes ending incarceration for drug use, decreasing the prison population, and reforming policing practices. Voting rights protection, combating voter suppression, and ensuring a diverse judiciary are also prioritized. The plan promises to fight environmental injustices and involve African Americans in the green economy. The "10-20-30" initiative targets long-term poverty in predominantly Black areas, while labor reforms aim to eliminate wage gaps and promote fair labor practices, with support for affordable childcare and education.

Strengths: Joe Biden's equity advancement plan's strengths lie in its comprehensive approach to tackling the systemic challenges faced by African Americans. Economically, it promises to enhance Black business growth and reduce wealth gaps. Education aims for affordable and accessible learning, potentially uplifting long-term economic prospects. Healthcare reforms seek to close disparity gaps, improving overall community health. Criminal justice changes are set to curb disproportionate incarceration rates among African Americans, particularly for non-violent offenses.

The plan's defense of voting rights aims to ensure fair political representation, while environmental justice efforts focus on including African Americans in the green economy. The "10-20-30" initiative has the potential to significantly aid impoverished communities and usher in labor reforms proposed to address wage gaps and strengthen worker protections, underpinning economic stability. Collectively, these measures are intended to dismantle barriers and promote equity.

Challenges: President Biden's plan's effectiveness depends on its implementation details. The plan proposes economic support for Black businesses and aims to bridge homeownership and educational funding gaps, yet it requires more specific execution strategies. Criminal justice reforms emphasize decriminalization of drug use and addressing police misconduct, but policy details are vague. Voting rights protection is prioritized, but the proposed strategies to fight suppression need further clarification.

The Plan's Environmental initiatives lack a clear action plan, and while the "10-20-30" approach to wealth disparity shows promise, a detailed wealth distribution roadmap is necessary. Labor reforms to eliminate pay gaps and strengthen protections are crucial, yet detailed implementation plans are missing. The plan's integrated approach to racial inequality needs clearer funding and execution details to ensure sustainability and independence from external political factors, with provisions to maintain momentum beyond the current administration for enduring change.

Feasibility: Joe Biden's equity plan faces significant obstacles, including legislative gridlock that could hinder policy passage, budget concerns due to its broad scope, and a lack of detailed policy outlines that complicate effective issue resolution. Administrative delays and political opposition, notably regarding criminal justice and voting rights reforms, present further challenges. The plan's permanence is uncertain without strategies to embed policies past the current term. Community-driven engagement is essential to the plan's success, ensuring African American voices guide and sustain the initiatives. Overall, while the plan targets critical concerns, its impact hinges on precise policy crafting and a solid execution framework, necessitating active collaboration with both lawmakers and the African American community.

The Black Policy Agenda for the State of the Union - The NAACP - 2024

The National Association for the Advancement of Colored People (NAACP) has historically championed civil rights and equality for Black Americans. Their policy agenda for the 2024 term addresses critical issues facing the Black community and emphasizes the need for systemic change. The NAACP's agenda centers on crucial policy priorities to advance racial justice and equality. They advocate for reforms to protect voting rights, emphasizing the importance of safe and accessible elections. The passage of the John Lewis Voting Rights Advancement Act is a crucial focus to restore critical protections for voting rights and safeguard democracy. Additionally, the NAACP highlights the need for economic equity, calling for a living wage for all Americans, particularly Black workers disproportionately affected by economic disparities. They stress the importance of regulating technology to protect workers' rights and address the impact of artificial intelligence on the workforce.

Furthermore, the NAACP emphasizes comprehensive police reform and criminal justice reform, including ending qualified immunity and implementing enhanced training to eliminate bias in policing. They advocate for transparent policing practices and safeguards against discriminatory use of artificial intelligence in law enforcement. Additionally, the NAACP highlights the impact of the Medicaid Unwinding crisis on communities of color and urges the federal government to address healthcare disparities by preserving Medicaid coverage and ensuring equitable access to healthcare for all Americans. Lastly, they stress the importance of equitable education policies that acknowledge and address the contributions and struggles of Black Americans, advocating against efforts to rewrite history and remove diversity standards in education.

Strengths: The NAACP's policy agenda embodies a steadfast dedication to advancing racial justice and equality. Its emphasis on voting rights, economic equity, policing reform, healthcare access, and education resonates deeply with the Black community's most urgent concerns. By contextualizing its policy recommendations in light of contemporary events and persistent threats, the NAACP exhibits a proactive stance toward confronting systemic challenges head-on.

Challenges: Implementing the NAACP's agenda necessitates forging unlikely bipartisan cooperation, enacting legislative measures, and sustaining advocacy endeavors. However, overcoming resistance from political adversaries and navigating intricate policy terrains could pose formidable challenges. Thus, ensuring accountability and devising mechanisms to gauge the efficacy of policy interventions are imperative for monitoring progress and effectively addressing emergent obstacles.

Feasibility: The feasibility of the NAACP's agenda hinges on a multitude of factors, encompassing political will, public backing, and institutional capabilities. To propel pivotal policy objectives forward, the organization must prioritize the establishment of coalitions, the mobilization of grassroots support, and the utilization of strategic alliances. Moreover, flexibility, adaptability, and unwavering persistence will emerge as indispensable attributes for adeptly maneuvering through the ever-evolving political terrain and effectuating substantive transformations.

The Long-Term Strategic Plan for Black America - Coalition of African American Leaders - 2023

The Long-Term Strategic Plan (LTSP) for Black America, crafted under the leadership of Baba Laurence Tunsill and a diverse panel of grassroots activists, represents a bold vision for the socioeconomic transformation of Black communities over a century. Rooted in Afrocentric principles and a commitment to self-reliance, the LTSP seeks to navigate Black America from a history of external imposition to a future characterized by autonomy and prosperity. Through a systematic approach encompassing nine critical sectors of governance, the plan endeavors to foster holistic well-being, economic empowerment, and cultural revitalization within existing Black American communities.

Strengths: The LTSP's strength lies in its comprehensive and inclusive approach to addressing Black America's multifaceted challenges. By embracing Afrocentric values and prioritizing self-determination, the plan resonates deeply with Black communities' aspirations and lived experiences, fostering a sense of ownership and agency in charting their collective destiny. Moreover, the phased implementation strategy spanning a century reflects a nuanced understanding of the complexities inherent in societal transformation, allowing for adaptive responses to evolving dynamics and entrenched structural barriers.

Challenges: Despite its ambitious vision and strategic framework, the LTSP faces several formidable challenges on the path to realization. Chief among these is the need to garner widespread support and sustained commitment from diverse stakeholders, including policymakers, community leaders, and the broader Black population. Overcoming entrenched systems of oppression, institutional inertia, and historical legacies of marginalization will require coordinated efforts and collective mobilization on an unprecedented scale. Additionally, the LTSP must contend with external pressures and potential backlash from entrenched interests resistant to transformative change, necessitating robust strategies for advocacy, coalition-building, and resilience.

Feasibility: The feasibility of the LTSP hinges on its ability to translate vision into actionable initiatives, navigate complex political landscapes, and secure the necessary resources and institutional support for implementation. While the distributed approach to self-reliance offers strategic advantages in terms of resilience and adaptability, it also presents logistical challenges in coordinating efforts across diverse communities and jurisdictions. Moreover, sustaining momentum and momentum over a century-long timeframe will require ongoing engagement, adaptive leadership, and a commitment to iterative learning and course correction. Nevertheless, the LTSP's potential to catalyze systemic change and foster transformative outcomes for Black America underscores its significance as a blueprint for long-term progress and empowerment.

The Vision for Black Lives - The Movement for Black Lives, 2024

The Movement for Black Lives (M4BL) offers a comprehensive and proactive approach to addressing systemic issues Black communities face through the "Vision for Black Lives." This initiative, supported by a broad coalition of over 50 organizations, articulates a future-oriented agenda to achieve Black liberation and equity. Launched initially in 2016 and updated in 2020, this platform covers a broad spectrum of policies intended to dismantle oppressive systems and promote justice across various sectors, including policing, economic equity, and health.

Strengths: The "Vision for Black Lives" demonstrates a robust intersectional approach, recognizing and addressing the nuanced challenges faced by the most marginalized within Black communities, such as women, queer, trans, and disabled individuals. The collaborative nature of the platform's development, involving numerous Black-led organizations, lends it a rich diversity of perspectives and a broad base of support, enhancing its legitimacy and resonance within the community. Moreover, the plan's adaptability, evidenced by its periodic updates, allows it to stay relevant in response to the evolving political and social landscape.

Challenges: Despite its comprehensive scope and collaborative foundation, the "Vision for Black Lives" faces significant hurdles in terms of implementation. Achieving the ambitious goals set out in the plan requires substantial changes at systemic and institutional levels, which may encounter resistance from existing power structures resistant to change. Additionally, the broad scope of the agenda could present challenges in maintaining focus and momentum across its various initiatives.

Feasibility: The feasibility of the "Vision for Black Lives" depends mainly on the political climate, availability of resources, and the sustained mobilization of grassroots and institutional support. While the plan outlines detailed policy steps and leverages a strong community base, translating these into actionable change will require overcoming significant political and societal barriers. Continuous engagement and strategic advocacy are essential to advance these policies, alongside building coalitions that can exert influence on policymakers and the public.

Comparative Analysis

The selected plans for developing sustainable Black communities share overarching objectives like economic empowerment, social justice, and political representation. However, the specific tactics and strategies they advocate can differ significantly. These differences are primarily influenced by the socio-political backgrounds, eras, ideologies, and personal experiences of the individuals or groups who developed the plans. Despite the differences in orientation, key themes can be identified between each plan and then utilized to fashion an improved comprehensive strategy.

For instance, the Black Panther Party's "10 Point Platform" called for sweeping reforms to address systemic racial injustices directly.

Similarly, contemporary plans like Ice Cube's "Contract with Black America" and the Movement for Black Lives (M4BL) "Vision for Black Lives" push for systemic changes with updated strategies that reflect current societal dynamics and issues.

The strengths across these plans often lie in their holistic approach to addressing multifaceted issues facing Black communities—incorporating economic, social, and political empowerment elements. For example, Amos Wilson's "Blueprint for Black Power" weaves together economic strategies with cultural and psychological upliftment, while Claud Anderson's "PowerNomics" focuses predominantly on economic autonomy and wealth creation within the community. The Long-Term Strategic Plan (LTSP) for Black America embraces Afrocentric values and prioritizes self-reliance, fostering a sense of ownership and agency within Black communities.

However, they all face a common challenge: transforming ambitious, broad-scope goals into actionable and sustainable outcomes. This is frequently compounded by the necessity of navigating complex political landscapes and overcoming significant resistance from established power structures. The Movement for Black Lives (M4BL) plan, with its intersectional approach and emphasis on community solidarity, exemplifies this challenge as it seeks to address both state violence and systemic injustices.

A critical variance among these plans is their strategic approaches and feasibility. For example, while the Black Panther Party adopted a more radical approach, focusing on self-defense and immediate demands, the Congressional Black Caucus operates within the existing political framework to push gradual legislative changes. Plans like Claud Anderson's "PowerNomics" and the LTSP focus predominantly on economic self-reliance and the creation of wealth within the community, which contrasts with broader political or social reform agendas seen in other plans.

Navigating through the realms of empowerment, Amos Wilson's "Blueprint for Black Power" offered a socio-economic vision that wove together economic strategies with the threads of cultural and psychological upliftment. In parallel, Claud Anderson's "PowerNomics" honed in on financial autonomy, prescribing tangible assets such as land and business ownership as the linchpins of social and political ascendancy, thus framing economic clout as the cornerstone of empowerment.

At the crossroads of activism and policy reform, Ice Cube's "Contract with Black America" unfurled a compendium of reforms targeting systemic injustices. However, the contract provided an aerial view without descending into the political trenches to map out a detailed path forward. In contrast, the Congressional Black Caucus (CBC) operated from within the political labyrinth, wielding a more pragmatic and perhaps realistic legislative pen, etching out policy changes tailored to the possible within the labyrinth's walls.

Election campaigns served as the backdrop for the introduction of Donald Trump's Platinum Plan and Joe Biden's "Lift Every Voice" plan. Trump's initiative, punctuated by its campaign-timed release, was met with cynicism and questioned for its sincerity and depth as it seemed to flirt with the objectives of electoral gains rather than the blueprint for systemic change. Biden's plan, while grand in its sweep, raised the specter of whether it was merely campaign trail oratory or if it harbored the seeds for genuine policy shifts.

The LTSP and M4BL's comprehensive plans reflect a long-term, systemic approach, emphasizing self-reliance, community empowerment, and intersectional justice. The LTSP's phased implementation strategy spanning a century and the M4BL's intersectional focus highlight their adaptability to evolving dynamics and entrenched structural barriers.

Examining these various strategic plans reveals the importance of a well-rounded approach that is adaptive to changing political and social climates. For future strategic developments, it is essential to learn from both the successes and shortcomings of past and present initiatives, building on them to formulate comprehensive, resilient strategies that can effectively address the challenges faced by Black communities. By incorporating a creative blend of direct action and legislative engagement, focusing on immediate and long-term goals, and ensuring inclusivity to address the needs of the most marginalized within the community, we can create a robust blueprint for the future. Additionally, acknowledging and planning for the resistance these initiatives might face is crucial, as is fostering broad community support and participation. This complex tapestry of approaches underscores the ongoing discourse on how best to realize the aspirations for a just and equitable society.

Conclusion

As we conclude this assessment, it becomes clear that no single plan offers a comprehensive solution; instead, it provides valuable lessons and perspectives. We can chart a more informed path forward by recognizing the common pitfalls of lacking specificity, political opposition, budget constraints, and the need for community engagement and sustainability. Future iterations of these plans must be characterized by precise policy proposals, broad-based political support, innovative resource allocation, and a steadfast commitment to the voices and needs of the communities they aim to empower. In this ongoing journey toward a more just and equitable America, the lessons learned from these plans serve as guiding stars, lighting the way for more impactful and sustainable change.

3

Anatomy of a Black Community: Understanding Social Capital, Resilience, and Sustainability

Introduction

Before developing an effective plan for Black communities, we must solidify our fundamental understanding of what makes a successful community. At their core, communities are social technology, vital for human survival and the augmentation of our living standards. These complex adaptive *social* systems are spaces where resources are pooled, burdens are shared, and cultural innovation thrives. It would not be an overstatement to assert that community is a fundamental building block of human civilization. The vitality of a community stems from its ability to consistently foster or attract new members who not only uphold the community's principles but also adapt to changing environmental realities (Bourdieu, 1986). A community thrives when it accomplishes these tasks effectively, thus enhancing the welfare and progress of its members (Folland, 2007).

However, when communities deviate from their foundational roles, it raises pivotal questions about the factors influencing their success or failure. To untangle these issues, we must dive into the concept of social capital, a significant factor in community development.

Social Capital: The Fabric of a Community

Social capital describes a community's nervous system or social infrastructure. It symbolizes the relationships, trust, and interconnectedness that bind people together, producing a formidable force for collective action (Hyyppa, 2010). This shared solidarity and common purpose empower communities to triumph over adversity (Jordan, 2014; Aldrich & Meyer, 2015; Menka & Ryan, 2012).

In simpler terms, social capital is the catalyst that transforms neighbors into family, unity into strength, and communities into unyielding support networks (Lin, 2008; Ravanera & Rajulton, 2010). It is the power that emerges when individuals unite, realizing that their collective strength surpasses their individual might (Palmer R. T., 2010).

Far from being a mere theoretical concept, social capital is crucial for community development (Newman, 2010). It facilitates community cooperation, collaboration, and progress (Putnam, 1993). Communities with substantial social capital witness their members actively participating in activities that elevate the community. This communal spirit manifests in building schools, supporting local businesses, and advocating for justice (Portes, 1998; Cornwell & Cornwell, 2008). In this way, social capital breathes life into a community, allowing for resiliency and strength.

Social capital can be categorized into three types: bonding, bridging, and linking. Bonding social capital is defined by the networks connecting family members, ethnic groups, social classes, and other close social groupings (Putnam, 2000). Bridging social capital is best understood as the ability of groups to form coalitions with other groups (Blair & Carroll, 2008). Linking social capital pertains to an individual's ability to establish and maintain relationships with various institutions and individuals, activating political and social power (Hawkins & Maurer, 2010).

In his seminal work "Bowling Alone: The Collapse and Revival of American Community" (2000), Robert Putnam explained the transformative power of social capital. He detailed how social capital nurtures civic engagement, social trust, and overall community well-being. Putnam's findings suggest that by fostering social capital, communities sow the seeds for economic prosperity, improved public health, and social cohesion (Blair & Carroll, 2008). Ultimately, social capital is the social fabric that connects individuals, spurring them to support one another and aspire for social change. Its importance lies in facilitating collaboration and progress and in its ability to advance sustainability and resilience.

Interplay Between Social Capital and Community Sustainability

Social capital is indispensable in driving sustainable development, underpinning community engagement, and consensus-building, which are critical to the efficacy of sustainability initiatives. It mobilizes communities to collaboratively address critical issues, from advocating for improved public services to conserving natural resources and spurring economic development. The shared bonds, trust, and connections extend community influence beyond local confines, granting access to a broader array of resources and opportunities and thus markedly improving the prospects for enduring community welfare.

Social capital intersects with each dimension of sustainability, bolstering economic sustainability by stimulating the development of networks that catalyze trade, entrepreneurship, and innovation. Furthermore, social capital supports environmental sustainability through a shared commitment to resource stewardship, and it undergirds social sustainability by reinforcing community resilience, facilitating inclusive governance, and participatory decision-making (McKenzie, 2004). Social capital is not merely a mechanism for achieving sustainability but also a critical indicator of a sustainably functioning society, where economic progress, environmental responsibility, and social well-being are harmoniously intertwined, safeguarding the resilience of society and the planet for the long haul.

Social sustainability is integral to social equality and demands the creation of societies characterized by fairness, vitality, health, community solidarity, and justice. A socially sustainable community is committed to developing resilient societal systems that equitably serve the present and future generations, ensuring universal access to essential services like education and healthcare, upholding cultural identities, and nurturing spaces for collective advancement and fulfillment (McKenzie, 2004).

The sphere of social sustainability, deeply intertwined with social capital, touches upon the responsibilities of businesses and charitable organizations within society, the dynamics of community relations, and the cultivation of supportive networks. It emphasizes how social capital facilitates the exchange of information, coordinates collaborative efforts, and enhances collective decision-making. The role of experts within social networks, as discussed by Cornwell & Cornwell (2008), emphasizes the advantage of specialized knowledge accessible through these relationships, providing a strategic benefit to communities.

Community participation and consensus are foundational to environmental planning and the success of sustainable development. Selman (2010) demonstrated that the effectiveness of such initiatives is significantly heightened by the presence of robust social capital, which cultivates trust, cooperation, and active involvement within communities.

Broska (2021) elucidated that sustainable community projects are born from a complex interplay of social needs, capital, norms, and environmental consciousness. Broska asserts that even individuals with minimal ecological concern can be inspired to act when influenced by a community's collective ethos. Broska's findings were consistent with Giacovelli's (2022) examination of social capital in energy transitions, which revealed a spectrum of impacts and underscored the need for deeper investigation into these dynamics.

Philanthropic behavior has also been linked to social capital, with studies by Graddy and Wang (2009) and Brown & Ferris (2007) demonstrating how donations and volunteering are augmented in communities where trust and social networks are robust. The importance of social capital also extends to volunteer caregiving, as shown in Baik, Crittenden, & Coleman's (2023) study, which posits that caregivers are more likely to volunteer when embedded in supportive and engaged community networks.

A consensus across academic research postulates that a deep understanding and deliberate cultivation of social capital are paramount for sustaining communities and reaching long-term sustainability objectives. This compelling connection between social capital and community sustainability underscores the vital role of social capital as an active force, empowering communities to navigate adversities and thrive amidst challenges. Historical evidence and scholarly discourse establish social capital as more than a theoretical construct; it is a palpable force that enables communities to craft a sustainable and resilient future. The evidence should encourage practitioners and policymakers to invest in cultivating social capital as a strategic imperative, ensuring the successful realization of sustainable community development.

Unearthing the Connection Between Social Capital and Community Resilience

Community resilience, the ability to rebound and learn from adversities, is intimately tied to social capital. Meerow, Newell, & Stults (2016) defined resilience as the capacity of a system to maintain or return to desired functions in the face of disturbances, adapt to changes, and transform systems limiting current or future adaptive potential. The litany of literature on social capital illuminates its deep connection with community resilience.

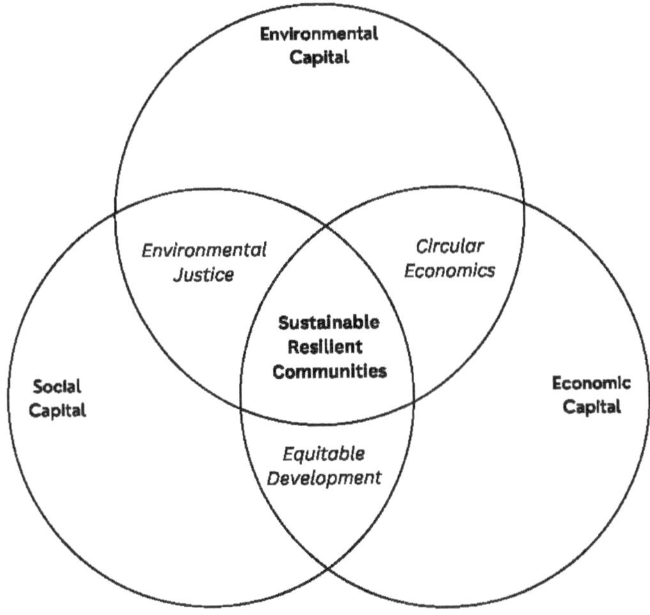

Figure 1: Conceptual Model of Sustainable and Resilient
Communities

Social capital is instrumental in building community resilience, as seen in communities' capacity to withstand and bounce back from adversities. Aldrich (2012) highlights this in his assertion that the real power for post-disaster recovery lies not in the built environment but in a community's social infrastructure—the preexisting network of relationships that foster trust and cooperation. These social ties are foundational for an organized, swift, and equitable recovery process.

The case of Hurricane María in Puerto Rico, as studied by Roque, Pijawka, and Wutich (2020), unveils that the three critical social capital dimensions—bonding, bridging, and linking—are instrumental in not just recovery but in fortifying communities against future disasters. These dimensions reflect shared values, expanded networks, new partnerships, and a collective resolve toward resilience.

Studies, including Menka and Ryan's (2012) examination of wildfire resilience, as well as investigations of the experiences following

Hurricane Katrina, as analyzed by Torres, Marshall, & Sydnor (2019), echo this sentiment, showing how communities rich in social capital harness collective action, share resources, and reinforce community bonds in the aftermath of a disaster. Hawkins and Maurer (2010) and Pyles and Cross (2008) further corroborate that family support during survival and the rebuilding phase exemplifies the utility of bonding social capital.

This is not isolated to individual cases; global and local initiatives, such as the United Nations Sustainable Development Goals, and community-specific projects, like the LA County Community Disaster Resilience project, underscore the recognition and integration of social capital into resilience-building strategies. These initiatives emphasize the necessity of harnessing local knowledge, engaging communities, and fostering continuous social learning.

The interplay between social capital and resilience is also evident in economic and health domains. Woolley et al. (2008) observed that communities with robust social capital are more economically resilient and support better academic outcomes for youth. Hutchinson et al. (2009) found a correlation between high social capital levels and lower mortality rates in Philadelphia, indicating the critical role of social networks in promoting health resilience.

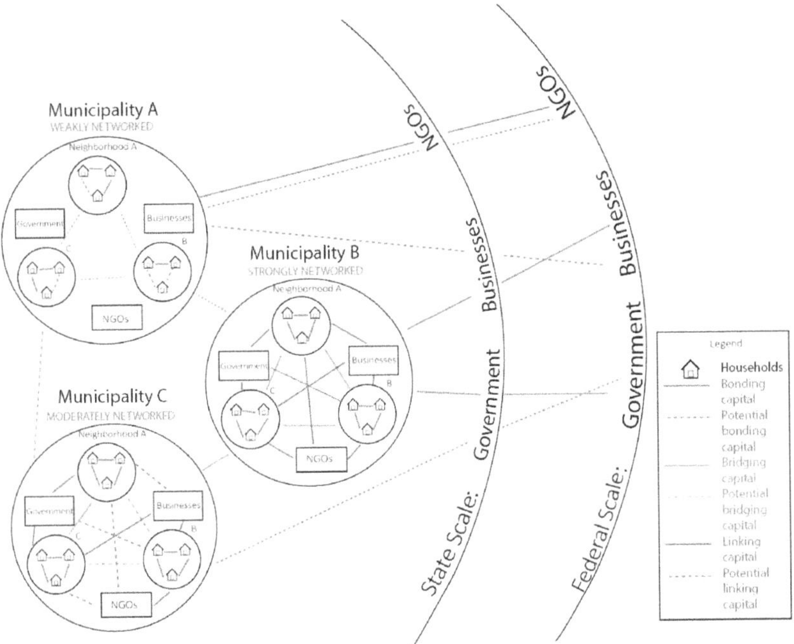

Figure 2: Conceptual diagram of actors and networks with varying strengths of social capital at different scales.

Thus, the literature firmly establishes that social capital, with its complex interpersonal and inter-organizational networks, is a cornerstone of community resilience. Aldrich suggests that the research should drive investment in community social infrastructure. The culture of preparedness, sustained by these networks, is now central to effective disaster management and long-term community well-being. This speaks volumes about the need to invest in the social capital of African American communities.

Social Capital and Black Communities: A Historical Perspective

Historically, the Black community has drawn strength from the power of social capital (Orr, 1999; Nembhard, 2014). The history of African Americans offers a litany of examples where extensive social networks and cooperation have proven to be a beacon of resilience amid systemic adversity (Carson, Lapsansky-Werner, & Nash, 2018).

The Underground Railroad epitomized linking social capital in action. It was a network of safe houses connecting White Americans and free Black Americans who risked their lives to assist formerly enslaved Black Men and Women in escaping slavery and acquiring freedom.

On the other hand, Tulsa, Oklahoma's Greenwood District, affectionately known as Black Wall Street, manifested the might of bonding social capital in the economic realm. Despite pervasive systemic racism, African American entrepreneurs and community leaders united to create a prosperous, self-sufficient community. Tulsa was one of many examples of free black communities that were established via economic collaboration and internal support.

The Harlem Renaissance is another example of social capital in post-civil war America. In many circumstances, African Americans leveraged their social capital to establish thriving businesses, own properties, and cultivate a sense of unity and pride. These historical events underline the transformative potential of social capital in fostering community development.

Dr. Jessica Gordon Nembhard's seminal work *Collective Courage: A History of African American Cooperative Economic Thought and Practice* (2014) depicts the long and rich history of cooperative business ownership and economic practices among African Americans from slavery to the present. African American communities have utilized collective economics, including but not limited to mutual aid societies, credit unions, and cooperative groceries, to create self-sufficient and autonomous economic institutions integral to their resistance and survival. These practices were a response to systemic racism and exclusion from the mainstream economy and provided a foundation for fiscal stability and community development. This is a primary example of the value of bonding social capital in Black America.

The Civil Rights Movement also offers a wealth of examples demonstrating the power of social capital. Civil rights activist Fannie Lou Hamer emphasized the interconnectedness inherent in social capital when she famously stated, "Nobody's free until everybody's free." Her words highlight the essence of community solidarity, emphasizing the collective strength required to withstand systemic oppression.

Black Organizations: The Foundations of Black Social Capital

Historically, Black organizations have showcased the power of collective engagement and social capital in improving the quality of life in Black communities, even in adversity. As a response to racism, African Americans created parallel institutions to generate the necessary levels of social capital to advance their causes. These organizations focused on racial pride, economic self-sufficiency, political autonomy, and racial justice, laying the groundwork for developing social infrastructure within Black communities.

Black Religious Institutions

Black religious institutions have been a bedrock of social capital. Born in an era of slavery and segregation, these Black survival organizations became the first sanctuaries of mutual aid and social interaction for African Americans, often being the only spaces for them to gather unsupervised. Their role evolved in response to the changing nature of White supremacy. That role matured during the mass movement for civil rights, becoming a platform for political activism and offering solace amidst racial animosity. Leaders like Martin Luther King Jr. leveraged their influence to inspire change from their pulpits. Today, Black religious institutions extend their reach to health, education, and community services, remaining a crucial community support structure.

The African Methodist Episcopal (AME) Church, initiated by Richard Allen in 1816, is a prime example of this enduring social capital. Allen, a former slave, launched the AME Church as the first African-American-led denomination in the U.S., marking a profound stride for an independent black religious entity. The AME Church also established Mutual Aid Societies, which offered support in times of hardship, such as assisting the sick, providing for burials, and offering financial aid. These societies became a lifeline for African Americans, fostering unity and resilience. These institutions, created by Allen, the AME Church, and Mutual Aid Societies, were critical centers of bonding social capital. They offered spiritual sustenance and a network of social and financial aid. Their existence allowed African Americans to pool resources, provide mutual assistance, and devise strategies against systemic racism. Today, Allen's legacy is continued through the AME Church and the various remnants of mutual aid programs employed in Black communities, highlighting the power of social capital in community empowerment and social change.

Historically Black Colleges and Universities (HBCUs)

HBCUs have also contributed substantially to developing social capital within African American communities. Established when access to higher education was critically limited for African Americans, HBCUs emerged as powerful institutions. Palmer and Gasman's (2008) study on HBCU graduates illuminates the profound impact of these universities in fostering social capital.

HBCUs empower individuals to overcome adversity and succeed by offering access to education, mentorship, and a supportive network. The robust alumni networks from these institutions further strengthen community bonds, offering platforms for mutual assistance and professional growth. The enduring significance of HBCUs and their graduates' contributions across various societal sectors underscores the institutions' pivotal role.

The Universal Negro Improvement Association (UNIA):

The UNIA, founded and led by Marcus Garvey in 1914, was a paramount social capital-producing institution in Black America. Its mission centered on empowering African Americans through economic independence, cultural pride, and the creation of global Black unity.

Garvey's UNIA generated "bonding social capital" through targeted efforts to foster a solid sense of identity and mutual support among African Americans. This allowed the organization to build a solid foundation of social trust, critical for collective action and resilience in the face of adversity. It peaked in the mid-1920s with an extensive network exceeding 3.5 million African Americans organized into hundreds of chapters. The UNIA's initiatives in entrepreneurship, such as the Black Star Line, a shipping company established by Marcus Garvey in 1919, aimed to economically link African Americans and the global African diaspora, offering tangible avenues for community development and wealth creation. This expanded "network capacity" enabled African Americans to access a broader range of resources and information, thus enhancing their social and economic potential. This emphasis on economic self-sufficiency was pivotal in shaping the community development and empowerment strategies that would influence subsequent generations and movements.

The Nation of Islam (NOI)

The NOI has been pivotal in cultivating bonding social capital among African American communities, most notably during the tumultuous 1960s. As a religious and social movement, the NOI focused on empowering African Americans, emphasizing self-sufficiency and economic independence, and establishing a strong community identity separate from the dominant white society. The organization's programs often led to the creation of schools, businesses, and social services, most notably their addiction counseling services, which benefited African American communities and contributed significantly to enhanced network capacity within them.

Moreover, the NOI's efforts extended to creating bridging social capital, connecting African Americans with broader networks that transcended their immediate social circles. This bridging of communities facilitated the exchange of ideas and resources vital in the push for civil rights and self-determination. The NOI's commitment to fostering social trust and agency within its ranks fortified its members against societal exclusion and played a crucial role in the broader movement for racial equality and pride.

Ubuntu: Examples of Contemporary Black Social Capital

Present-day community service organizations continue the legacy of those from previous generations. They harness the power of social capital through grassroots organizing, community engagement, and advocacy campaigns. Using modern technology and lessons from traditional grassroots organizing efforts, these organizations are the first line of defense in the contemporary struggle against racism and the torchbearers illuminating the path to Black Sustainability. This is not an exhaustive list of such organizations but a contracted list of those with whom I have had the privilege to study and collaborate.

The Dream Defenders

The Dream Defenders is an organization of activists formed in the aftermath of Trayvon Martin's murder in 2012. This organization has become a crucial part of the contemporary human rights movement, focusing on mobilizing Black and Brown youth toward building a society that prioritizes healthcare, housing, and employment while resisting mass incarceration and militarization. Their efforts have brought attention to various issues ranging from systemic racism in the criminal justice system to broader societal inequalities.

The group is known for bold and direct actions, such as occupying the Florida State Capitol to protest the "Stand Your Ground" law. Although they failed to change the law, their activism laid the foundation for a resurgence in youth-led civil rights advocacy in Florida. Today, The Dream Defenders continue to advocate for the abolition of prisons and police as part of a broader struggle against systemic control, oppression, and capitalism, emphasizing the need for community-led alternatives to dealing with harm and violence through transformative justice.

The Dream Defenders embody Black feminist principles, actively combating violence and oppression while prioritizing efforts to address the intersectional violence faced by Black women. Their mission extends beyond opposing physical prisons to challenging the societal structures that reinforce inequality and systemic punishment. Embracing a socialist framework, they advocate for a cooperative society that prioritizes meeting the needs of all people over the profit-driven desires of the wealthy elite. Rejecting the notion of liberation through Black capitalism, they emphasize the importance of a system that guarantees basic needs for everyone. On an international scale, they stand in solidarity with oppressed peoples worldwide, opposing all forms of racism and bigotry. Recognizing their struggles as interconnected with global issues, they call attention to the shared exploitation perpetuated by powerful corporations and the military-industrial complex.

Essentially, the Dream Defenders champion a transformative vision for a society where equality, justice, and mutual support replace exploitation, incarceration, and capitalist-driven inequality. They call for comprehensive societal reform that uplifts all marginalized communities domestically and globally.

The National Black Food Justice Alliance (NBFJA)

The NBFJA is a coalition dedicated to advancing black food sovereignty, which is the right and capability of Black communities to control their food systems, including production and distribution methods. They emphasize governance over these systems, advocating for a food economy where Black individuals and communities exercise autonomy over food that is healthy, culturally appropriate, and sustainably produced. NBFJA underscores the need for action to assert these rights, advocating for a shift away from corporate dependency towards community-based power and self-determination.

The Alliance also champions the development of self-sustaining food economies, recognizing the historical extraction of Black wealth and labor to prop up a predominantly white, corporate-controlled food industry. They promote models of Black ownership and alternative economic structures, such as cooperatives, which allow communities to reclaim and benefit directly from their labor and businesses.

Additionally, the NBFJA addresses land justice, stressing the importance of land as the foundation of sovereignty and revolution. They confront displacement and work to reclaim and liberate land to restore the relationship between Black communities and the natural environment. This connection is agricultural, spiritual, economic, cultural, and communal. The Alliance's work is thus deeply rooted in healing and empowerment.

Harambe House Inc. / Citizens for Environmental Justice (HH/CFEJ):

HH/CFEJ in Savannah, Georgia, has also played a pivotal role in fostering social capital. Harambee House is a non-profit organization based in Savannah, Georgia, committed to pursuing environmental justice and advancing social change. Established in 1990, HH/CFEJ has been influential in advocating for civic engagement and empowering communities to take collective action. HH/CFEJ focuses on helping individuals, especially the youth, to find their voice and develop leadership skills, functioning as a catalyst for community transformation.

Their approach includes collaboration with diverse stakeholders, including academic institutions, government bodies, businesses, and community groups, to enhance partnerships and promote an integrated approach to community development. They strongly emphasize integrity and excellence in their service to the community.

HH/CFEJ has been actively involved in projects like Tools for Change – Savannah, employing Community-based Participatory Research (CBPR) to investigate the relationship between violence and environmental factors. They address local environmental health hazards like air pollution, lead, asbestos, and mold, providing necessary training and resources for hazard containment, remediation, and environmental cleanup.

The HH/CFEJ cultivates social cohesion and collective engagement among Black residents through cultural events, community forums, and economic empowerment workshops. HH/CFEJ builds resilient communities by equipping them with knowledge and skills pertinent to environmental justice and health, fostering a proactive stance on social issues and ecological stewardship well into the future.

Cooperation Jackson

Cooperation Jackson is an initiative dedicated to creating economic democracy and fostering community ownership in Jackson, Mississippi. Its strategy is to build a cooperative network of worker cooperatives, a business incubator, an educational center named the Kuwasi Balagoon Center for Economic Democracy and Development, and a cooperative financial institution. Its focus is mobilizing the structurally underemployed, particularly in Black and Latino communities, to establish democratically owned cooperatives to transform the economy and society.

In protest of competitive capitalism, the organization aims to promote a solidarity economy based on collective ownership, self-management, and sustainable practices. This includes providing comprehensive education and support for residents to start and manage cooperative businesses to create jobs that offer stability, fair wages, and benefits. Rooted in decades of struggle for democratic rights and economic justice, especially for African Americans in the South, Cooperation Jackson envisions a model of economic organization that prioritizes people and the planet over profit, aiming to inspire and replicate this model in other regions.

Low Country Alliance for Model Communities (LAMC)

LAMC, established in 2005, is a community-driven organization rooted in North Charleston, South Carolina. With a vision to enhance the living standards of neighborhood residents, LAMC has been steadfast in building a framework for healthy family environments. Their strategic focus is spread across four pivotal sectors. In affordable housing, LAMC has forged strong partnerships to offer accessible living options to residents, addressing the growing need for housing that does not burden low-income families. On the economic front, the organization has been proactive in initiating programs that stimulate economic growth and viability within its target areas, providing a foundation for prosperity and community development.

LAMC also places a high value on education, striving to bridge gaps and dismantle barriers that residents from low-wealth communities often face in pursuit of knowledge and skills. Through collaborative educational initiatives, LAMC empowers individuals with the resources needed to thrive academically. In the realm of environmental justice, the organization is committed to raising awareness among local leaders, residents, and students about the principles of environmental equity. LAMC actively addresses the concerns of legacy pollution, advocating for a cleaner and more just environment. Through these four core pillars, LAMC has established itself as a catalyst for transformative change, breaking the cycle of poverty and fostering opportunities for all community members.

Citizens for A Sustainable Future, Inc. (CSF)

CSF is a nonprofit think tank and action-oriented organization based in Tallahassee, Florida. It advocates for sustainable living practices and environmental justice within African American communities. CSF was founded in 2012 by a team of academics and activists as part of an effort to design creative and sustainable solutions to enhance the quality of life for Black communities.

CSF focuses on addressing the specific challenges that African-American communities face, such as environmental racism and the resulting impacts on their social and economic stability, which in turn affects their environmental resilience. Many of their programs and interventions raise awareness and enhance the organization in Black communities by developing partnerships and increasing community engagement through various programs and initiatives. Their programming includes collective civic engagement efforts to organize and inform voters as they participate in local politics. In addition, CSF works to enhance community resilience and advance environmental justice through youth empowerment efforts coupled with cultural celebration events.

Groundwork USA: Jacksonville and New Orleans

The Groundwork USA network demonstrates how national organizations can engage deeply with Black communities to foster social capital through community-driven environmental and social initiatives. With a mission to regenerate physical environments while promoting equity, civic engagement, and sustainability, Groundwork USA's localized approach ensures its work resonates with each community's unique challenges and strengths. Two examples of this work are Groundwork Jacksonville in Florida and Groundwork New Orleans in Louisiana, where robust community engagement is central to advancing social capital in Black communities.

Groundwork Jacksonville is vital in revitalizing historic Black neighborhoods in Jacksonville, Florida. By cleaning up urban creeks, repurposing contaminated lands, and leading the development of the Emerald Trail, Groundwork Jacksonville engages residents, business leaders, and funders to shape their environment collaboratively. They foster trust and build community pride by providing resources to community leaders, allowing for meaningful involvement in their neighborhood development. In recent work with local community organizations, they have made an earnest effort to offset potential displacement resulting from infrastructure improvements by co-creating a home repair program in a gentrification-prone Black neighborhood that assists residents with property taxes while providing climate mitigation improvements such as cool roofs and rain gardens. Their emphasis on "doing with" rather than "doing for" is their method of ensuring that the residents most affected by environmental challenges are not just participants but leaders in the process, cultivating a shared sense of ownership and leadership within the community.

Groundwork New Orleans, established in the aftermath of Hurricane Katrina, exemplifies resilience and innovation in building social capital. Their numerous community projects, including rain gardens, bioswales, and their Earth Lab outdoor classroom, are utilized to empower residents to address stormwater management and ecological restoration, which are vital for the city's recovery. Groundwork New Orleans emphasizes skill-building, community leadership, and service learning, mainly through its Green Team program, which engages youth in environmental stewardship and civic action. By working in historically underserved areas such as the Lower Ninth Ward and Central City, the organization brings residents together to tackle shared challenges, reinforcing collective identity and solidarity.

Both Groundwork Jacksonville and Groundwork New Orleans illustrate how national networks can adapt their frameworks to meet local needs, fostering social capital by empowering Black communities to shape their environments. These organizations address environmental and infrastructural challenges and create platforms for collaboration, leadership, and community pride, ensuring their impact is sustainable and far-reaching.

Social Capital at play in the contemporary Black Community

Social capital represents a tapestry of resilience and communal fortitude in the African American community. It is an invaluable resource, facilitating mutual support and unity and catalyzing social and political mobilization (Liu, Austin, & Orey, 2009). The influence of social structures such as the "politicized black church" extends beyond immediate communal bounds, fostering civic engagement and broader societal involvement (McKenzie, 2008).

Academic institutions, particularly Historically Black Colleges and Universities (HBCUs), continue to exemplify the nurturing environments that bolster social capital among African American students, contributing to their educational success (Palmer & Gasman, 2008). Meanwhile, in African American urban communities, robust social ties correlate with enhanced educational outcomes for children, highlighting the critical role of social support in academic achievement (Woolley et al., 2008).

Moreover, the interplay between social capital and mental health is a significant impact area. Social networks within these communities demonstrate a "buffering effect," mitigating the adverse effects of depression and fostering mental resilience among African American students (Fitzpatrick et al., 2005). This buffering capacity is especially pronounced in interventions designed to combat maternal depression in violence-prone urban settings (Lewin et al., 2011).

Yet, the benefits of social capital are not uniformly distributed. Structural barriers and the racial makeup of neighborhoods markedly influence the power of social ties. Research by Hutchinson et al. (2009) underscores the pronounced health benefits in predominantly black neighborhoods with substantial social capital, as evidenced by lower all-cause mortality rates. However, skepticism persists within

Black communities about the ability to overcome entrenched systemic challenges, suggesting a nuanced interplay between social capital and structural conditions (Hobson-Prater & Leech, 2011).

To this end, Gilbert & Dean (2013) called for a more profound integration of race into social capital and health discourse, advocating for an approach recognizing the unique forms of social capital forged within African American communities. These forms of capital are not merely survival mechanisms but potent tools for combating systemic oppression and fostering health equity.

Gilbert et al. (2022) argue that addressing the impact of structural racism on the development and utilization of social capital is paramount. A race-conscious social capital framework informed by Black experiences is vital for advancing racial justice and social progress.

Ultimately, the body of literature affirms that social capital is both a product of and a prerequisite for sustainable community development and resilience (Aldrich & Meyer, 2015; Selman, 2010). To harness this capital effectively, there is an urgent need for scholarly and practical engagement that recognizes the complexities of race, acknowledges the power of community-driven networks, and fosters environments where social capital can thrive and enact transformative change.

The Dark Side of Social Capital

It is important to note that there are negative aspects of social capital. Social Capital can facilitate the sustainability of networks that detract from the larger community. Criminal organizations are one of many examples of the dark side of social capital. Social capital's impacts are intertwined with power dynamics. For instance, Aldrich (2015) discovered that strong social capital in one community could divert resources for disaster response from others.

Orr's research showed how social capital in Baltimore's White communities was able to stifle school reform efforts in Black areas. My case study research on majority Black communities further identified that while Black communities had adequate bonding social capital, they lacked the Bridging and Linking aspects, which were critical for the effectiveness of social change efforts (Strouble Jr., 2015). Hence, the elevation of social capital in vulnerable communities is particularly essential.

The Social Capital Imperative

From post-disaster recovery to educational institutions and community gardens, social capital has repeatedly proven its mettle. By recognizing the significance of social capital and actively promoting its development, communities can enhance their resilience and capacity to address challenges. Communities with strong social bonds are better equipped to respond to crises, support one another, and collectively work towards common goals (Aldrich D. P., 2012).

Some specific practices can be adopted to bolster social capital, such as incentivizing community participation, nurturing leadership, fostering trust and network development activities, and creating or revitalizing local organizations (Aldrich, 2015). Community gardens and other collective projects are exemplary methods for boosting social capital (Alaimo, Reischl, & Allen, 2010). The advent of social media and online communications offers a new frontier for raising social capital (Steinfield, DiMicco, Ellison, & Lampe, 2009). Social-cultural relations are the critical adhesive that binds a community together and boosts its resilience. Therefore, creating and cultivating social capital is paramount in building resilient and sustainable Black communities.

4

Black in "AmeriKKKa": Racial Oppression and its Impact on Black Communities

"Racism is the system of racial subjugation against non-whites in every area of human relations communication, education, labor, politics, law, religion, sex, war, and economics." Ras Kass

Introduction

This chapter explores the concept of racial oppression and its profound impact on Black communities. The aim is to provide a comprehensive understanding of racism by examining its definitions, types, and effects, drawing on lessons from African American History and Critical Race Theory (CRT). In this chapter, we embark on a thought-provoking discussion to uncover the roots of racism deeply embedded within the United States. By peeling back the layers of history, we aim to shed light on the systemic nature of racism and its enduring impact on Black communities. By peering into the mechanisms and consequences of racial oppression, we can gain insights into the challenges faced by Black communities in terms of social capital and community development. Furthermore, confronting these uncomfortable truths will allow for the strategic dismantling of oppressive systems in order to strive g for a more equitable and just future.

Key Definitions: Racism, White Supremacy, and White Privilege

The definition and function of racism remain subjects of intense debate within contemporary academic circles. While extensive research has been conducted on the topic, a consensus on a definitive definition remains elusive.

There are proponents defending the traditional definition found in dictionaries, which defines racism as the belief that race is the primary determinant of human traits and capacities, leading to an inherent superiority of a particular race. However, many scholars agree that this definition fails to capture the complexities of racism. Reducing racism to a simple "belief" presents significant problems as it mystifies racism and requires individuals identifying it to read the minds of racist actors. It is plausible that some slave owners and even members of the Ku

Klux Klan did not genuinely believe in racial superiority but instead sought to exploit situational opportunities for economic or political gains. However, regardless of their intentions or beliefs, their actions and behaviors still contributed to the same deleterious impact on the victims.

Popularly, racism is myopically conceptualized as the hatred of a person based on their race. While this component of racism, along with the belief in inherent superiority, is present, this definition is inadequate for the same reason. Racism is not solely an emotional or psychological phenomenon. If hating Black people were the extent of racism, it would not have had such a profound impact worldwide, affecting hundreds of millions of Black people for centuries.

While many race theorists acknowledge the limitations of traditional definitions, a divide remains in the community regarding the best approach to defining the phenomena. Some theorists build upon conventional definitions by adding the qualifier of power inequality (Sue, 2003; Tatum, 2007; Urquidez, 2020). They argue that racism is both the belief in superiority and the hatred of a person because of their phenotype, accompanied by the power to oppress. This definition brings us closer to a comprehensive understanding but still falls short.

The disproportionate power relationship criteria, although often true, is not all-encompassing and would hinder the identification of racism when power dynamics are unclear. Italy's invasion of Ethiopia in 1935 is an excellent example of this point. Italy aimed to seize control of Ethiopia's resources to improve its own economic conditions. Much of their decision to invade Ethiopia was also based on the phenotypical traits of Ethiopians (Du Bois, 1935). Therefore, the power dynamic would not negate the racist nature of the attack. Even if the countries had equal economic and military power, the attack would still be racist in orientation.

Before going deeper into the historical context and systemic barriers, it is crucial to establish clear definitions of a few key terms.

- White supremacy encompasses the ideologies and social arrangements that prioritize the interests of persons who are socially classified as White.
- White privilege denotes the unearned advantages and benefits that White individuals experience solely based on their race.

Understanding these definitions is essential for comprehending the dynamics of racial oppression and its effects on Black communities. Jones (2002) provides a comprehensive operational definition of racism as a system that structures opportunity and assigns value based on phenotype. This definition captures the systemic nature of racism and its impact on individuals and communities. Building upon this definition, my approach incorporates components from Bonilla-Silva (2013), Gee et al. (2009), and Jones (2002) to craft an operational definition of racism.

- Racism: the process, systems, collective ideologies, and behaviors that perpetuate racial inequality and afford privilege to a dominant racial group based on their phenotypical traits.

I offer this comprehensive definition as a means to incorporate the various aspects of racism with clear criteria. First, this definition focuses on the modes of transmission of racism and then on its impact on its victims and benefactors. Furthermore, this approach to defining racism captures the primary output of racism, which is racial stratification that creates marginalized groups and privileged groups. Using this comprehensive operational definition of racism, we can say what racism is and what it does, as well as who benefits and who suffers. From this point, we can appropriately measure racism and identify its actors without requiring knowledge of their "true feelings" or intentions. Ultimately, the qualifier is: if your practices contribute to the creation and or maintenance of racial inequality, you are participating in racism. This is a more nuanced understanding of racism and its intricate societal manifestations.

Using Critical Race Theory to Explain Racism

To comprehend the multifaceted nature of racism, it is crucial to adopt a framework that goes beyond traditional whiteness-centered definitions. Critical Race Theory (CRT) offers valuable insights into racism by analyzing the intersection of race, power, and privilege. CRT recognizes that racism is not just a matter of individual prejudice but, rather a systemic and structural issue deeply ingrained in society (Delgado & Stefancic, 2001). By acknowledging the pervasive influence of racism, CRT allows us to analyze the ways in which racial oppression operates at various levels.

Critical Race Theory (CRT) provides a valuable framework for examining social interaction in the United States from the perspective of oppressed minorities. The roots of CRT can be traced back to the works of scholars like Bell (1985, 1992) in the 1980s and '90s, who critiqued the slow pace of racial reform and the rollback of gains made during the civil rights movements of the 1960s (Delgado & Stefancic, 2013; Harris, 2012; Ladson-Billings, 2011). CRT gained momentum as critical legal studies scholars joined the movement, seeking new approaches to challenge the perceived perpetuation of racism in legal studies and American law (Crenshaw, 2011).

A central theme in early CRT literature is the assertion of inherent bias within American culture and the adverse impact of racism on the progress of non-White individuals in society (Bell, 1980; Crenshaw et al., 1995). As CRT evolved in scholarly literature, diverse groups of scholars and researchers began investigating the various components of racism in other social sciences (Delgado & Stefancic, 2012).

Over the course of 30 years of research, several key themes emerged within the CRT literature (Crenshaw, 2011; Delgado & Stefancic, 2012). In this section, seven identified themes constitute CRT's intellectual fabric.

The first overarching theme in CRT literature is the concept of the permanence of racism, suggesting that racism is normative behavior and a regular experience for people of color, thereby negatively influencing Black individuals and communities (Crenshaw et al., 1995; Delgado & Stefancic, 2012).

Interest convergence, also known as material determinism, is another crucial concept in CRT. It posits that racism benefits both elite and working-class Whites' social and political agendas, resulting in a lack of incentive for society to eradicate or mitigate racist practices. Action to reduce the effects of racism often occurs only when there is a shared interest between the victims and elite Whites (Bell, 1980; Bell, 1992; Delgado & Stefancic, 2012).

The social construction thesis is a significant concept for critical race theorists. It asserts that race is a social construct that dominant forces in society choose to disregard or promote based on their own interests. Within this framework, biological racial differences receive undue attention to support the interests of the dominant racial group (Crenshaw et al., 1995; Delgado & Stefancic, 2012).

Differential racialization is another recurring theme in CRT literature. It suggests that the dominant racial group racializes different minority groups differently based on the interests of the dominant group, leading to varying levels of favor or increased oppression for each racial group (Abrams & Molo, 2009; Delgado & Stefancic, 2012). This understanding informs the examination of social capital in majority Black communities compared to communities composed of a multiracial non-White majority.

The value of stories told by people of color due to their unique experiences with racism is emphasized in CRT literature. Some critical race theorists argue that these experiences qualify them as authorities on issues related to racism (Delgado & Stefancic, 2012). This perspective plays a crucial role in this research, focusing on information provided by African American community members.

Intersectionality, another aspect of CRT, recognizes the impact of social diversity on the experience of racism. It acknowledges that some groups may face multiple forms of oppression, and a narrow focus on race may overlook other sources of oppression related to gender, class, and sexual preference (Delgado & Stefancic, 2012).

Additionally, many CRT scholars reject several liberal conceptions, such as color blindness, objectivity, merit, formal equality, and post-racialism, in favor of a racial realism perspective (Bell, 1992; Bell, 2008; Crenshaw, 2011). Racial realism argues that racial equality as a goal of civil rights is unrealistic because the law and the state serve the interests of the dominant race in society. Failure to achieve racial equality is attributed to structural determinism, suggesting that our social and political systems are not adequately designed to address race-related issues (Delgado & Stefancic, 2012; Parks, 2008). Crenshaw (2011) further contends that the social and political systems themselves impede progress in race relations.

By incorporating these key themes of CRT into our analysis, we can deepen our understanding of how race, racism, and social dynamics impact Black communities and contribute to the development of more inclusive and transformative community practices.

Racism 101

It is crucial to recognize that the United States was founded on principles that perpetuated racism. From the formation of the thirteen British colonies, the pursuit of economic and political power for White individuals was prioritized, often at the expense of Indigenous Americans and African captives. The desire for land expansion and the consolidation of Whiteness played significant roles in shaping the nation's identity. The Constitutional Convention, a pivotal moment in American history, exposed the deeply embedded racism present in the nation's foundations. The exclusionary practices that limited participation to White men resulted in compromises that devalued and oppressed marginalized groups. From the 3/5ths Compromise to the delay in addressing the importation of enslaved Africans, these decisions laid the groundwork for racial inequality within the country's legal framework.

While progress has been made in the fight against racism, it is essential to acknowledge that it has not been eradicated. Racism has evolved and adapted, taking on more subtle and insidious forms. Its presence can be seen in various aspects of society, including education, healthcare, criminal justice, and economic opportunity. Systemic barriers continue to perpetuate racial disparities, hindering the advancement of marginalized communities.

Examining statistical data further illuminates the enduring impact of racism. Despite constituting a minority of the population, White men disproportionately hold positions of power and influence. This manufactured superiority is a consequence of prejudicial and discriminatory policies that consolidate privilege and suppress communities of color. The statistical disparities highlight the need for systemic change to address the underlying racial biases that perpetuate these inequalities.

Types of Racism

To fully comprehend the impact of racism, it is crucial to understand its various forms. Jones (2002) identifies three distinct types of racism: institutionalized racism, personally mediated racism, and internalized racism. Each of these forms contributes to the perpetuation of racial inequality and the marginalization of non-White racial groups.

Institutionalized racism refers to the organizational structures, procedures, and cultural norms that result in racially based disparities in accessing social, political, and human capital resources (Henkel, Dovidio, & Gaertner, 2006; Jones, 2002). This type of racism is deeply ingrained in societal institutions, including education, housing, employment, healthcare, and the legal system. It manifests through material wealth inequality and power imbalances, denying equal opportunities and reinforcing the dominance of the White racial group (Jones, 2002).

Personally mediated racism encompasses prejudice and discrimination exhibited by individuals toward others based on phenotype (Jones, 2002). This type of racism can take various forms, including acts of disrespect, suspicion, devaluation, and dehumanization (Jones, 2002). Personally mediated racism can be overt or covert, but its impact is equally harmful, perpetuating stereotypes and reinforcing racial hierarchies.

Furthermore, in examining personally mediated racism, research suggests that it generally falls into two categories (Gawronski, Peters, & Brochu, 2008; Pearson et al., 2009; Son Hing, Hamilton, & Zanna, 2008). The first category is explicit prejudice or conscious and deliberate negative evaluation of a different racial group based on memory and past experiences. The second category is implicit prejudice, which manifests as automatic negative associations of a distinct racial group without deliberation or intent (Son Hing et al., 2008).

Internalized racism is a consequence of racial oppression, wherein racially oppressed individuals internalize negative attitudes about their own abilities and worth (Jones, 2002; Pyke, 2010). It occurs when marginalized individuals accept the negative perceptions and stereotypes imposed by the dominant racial group (Pyke, 2010). Internalized racism leads to self-doubt, self-devaluation, and a sense of cultural inferiority, hindering the development of positive racial identity and impeding community empowerment (Speight, 2007). Ultimately, internalized racism can cause many to act as agents of White Supremacy, carrying out anti-BIPOC agendas, sometimes consciously and in many cases implicitly.

Black Racism?

The debate surrounding whether Black people can be racists is contentious, often stemming from differing perspectives on the nature and definition of racism. While some argue that racism is solely a system devoid of individual actors, this viewpoint fails to acknowledge that systems are fundamentally composed of social interactions carried out at the personal level.

Although African Americans, as a collective, cannot practice racism against Whites in the current social arrangement due to historical and contemporary power imbalances, it is important to recognize that they can engage in racist behavior toward non-White individuals with less power.

It is crucial to consider the consequences of racism and acknowledge that actors at various levels play a role in making decisions and carrying out actions that have harmful impacts on non-White individuals. Black people can indeed contribute to racism as proxy or "de facto" racists when they assume positions of authority within a racist system and participate in social interactions that perpetuate inequality and harm non-White people. In this context, skin color becomes irrelevant, as it is the actions and their resulting impact that determine whether an individual and their behaviors can be classified as racist.

Ultimately, those who actively work to structure and maintain local or global systems that create and uphold racial inequality and White supremacy can be considered racists, irrespective of their own racial background. This perspective highlights the importance of under-standing the role of individual agency within the broader framework of systemic racism and dismantling the structures that perpetuate racial injustice.

Historical Context: Old Fashioned Racism

To better understand the present, we must first examine the his-torical context in which racial oppression against Black communities originated. Throughout history, Black/African American communities have shown remarkable resilience and created parallel institutions due to exclusion from White institutions. However, the constant threat from White terrorism, such as lynching and violence, coupled with serial displacement and divestment, severely impacted the development of Black communities.

The systemic barriers imposed on Black communities have con-tributed to their marginalization and perpetuated racial oppression. Black Codes, enacted at the state and local levels, aimed to maintain White economic, social, and political supremacy. Wage theft and manipulation of credit scams trapped Black Southerners in perpetual debt and poverty, further exacerbating the racial wealth gap. Lynching served as a brutal mechanism to enforce White supremacy and discourage resistance. Disenfranchisement and voter intimidation through Jim Crow laws undermined the political power of Black communities. Additionally, mass incarceration, rooted in historical racial oppression, disproportionately affects Black individuals and perpetuates social and economic inequalities.

The Evolution of Racism

Racism has continually adapted and modified over time to meet the needs of its benefactors (Bonilla-Silva, 2013). Researchers describe old-fashioned racism as the more overt and explicit form of racism based on notions of biological supremacy and a desire for social distance between races (e.g., Gawronski et al., 2008; Tesler, 2013). This type of racism can be associated with explicit forms of discrimination. For instance, Tesler (2013) found that old-fashioned racist attitudes influenced policy and political decisions made by some Whites during the 2008 presidential election. Huddy and Feldman (2009) also used experimental methods to support their hypothesis that elements of old-fashioned racism correlated with political decisions among White participants.

Son Hing et al. (2008) conducted research on race and proposed a two-dimensional model to identify three typologies of racists: the modern racist, the principled conservative, and the aversive racist. Modern racists exhibit high levels of explicit prejudice along with high levels of implicit prejudice. However, unlike the old-fashioned racist, the modern racist does not embrace outright discrimination or bigotry but subscribes to more subtle discriminatory beliefs, such as claiming that racism no longer exists or that there is more racism against White people (Gawronski et al., 2008; Norton & Sommers, 2011). The principled conservative has high levels of explicit prejudice and low levels of implicit prejudice. For example, Renya, Korfmacher, and Tucker

(2005) suggested that the principled conservative opposes affirmative action that benefits African Americans more than affirmative action that benefits women. Lastly, the aversive racist exhibits low levels of explicit prejudice and high levels of implicit prejudice (Son Hing et al., 2008; Pearson et al., 2009).

Aversive racism is a subtle racism that is considered to have replaced traditional overt or old-fashioned racism, particularly among liberals (Bonilla-Silva, 2013; Pearson et al., 2009). Aversive racism, although often personally mediated, remains hidden behind the perpetrators' liberal or egalitarian views (Pearson, Dovidio, & Gaertner, 2009). In other words, aversive racists genuinely believe they are not practicing prejudice or discrimination, yet their actions subtly discriminate and have varying consequences (Pearson et al., 2009). Studies examining aversive racism have shown evidence of discrimination by Whites in employment or college admission applicant selection, as well as legal decisions (Pearson et al., 2009). These findings align with Pager's (2003) research, which revealed racially discriminatory hiring practices by employers, even when considering the criminal backgrounds of applicants.

While there are different types of racists, as Bonilla-Silva (2013) suggests, the objective of racism to maintain and enforce White supremacy remains the same. The tactics, however, have evolved over time. Due to demographic, social, political, and economic changes and increased agitation by African Americans during the Cold War and Civil Rights eras, changes to the old racial ideology were inevitable (Bonilla-Silva, 2013). This view aligns with Alexander's New Jim Crow thesis (2012), asserting that social control mechanisms used against African Americans have life spans, deaths, and rebirths to fit the political and social requirements of each era. For example, as slavery became socially unacceptable, Jim Crow became the new form of social control to maintain racial inequality. Subsequently, when Jim Crow was no longer socially acceptable, mass incarceration in a colorblind context became the latest method of social control (Alexander, 2012). The argument of critical race theorists that interest convergence is responsible for so-called improvements in race relations in the United States is consistent with this perspective.

Some scholars consider modern racism or the new racism as more subtle and sophisticated but just as effective and damaging as old-fashioned racism (Bonilla-Silva, 2013; Sue et al., 2007). In the modern context, people of color are less likely to encounter overt forms of exclusion and instead become targets of a range of micro-aggressive racist behaviors (Yosso et al., 2009; Sue et al., 2007). Microaggressions are "brief everyday exchanges that send denigrating messages to people of color" (Sue et al., 2007, p. 273). Yosso et al. (2009) and Sue et al. (2007) have conducted extensive research on racial microaggressions, which fall into three categories: micro-assaults or explicit racial derogation, micro-insults or offensive and insensitive communications that humiliate cultural customs and racial identity, and micro-invalidations, which disregard or invalidate a person's experiences or feelings regarding race-related issues.

This new racism functions to keep minorities in their places through increasingly covert means and the complete avoidance of racial terminology (Bonilla-Silva, 2013). Proponents of the latest and improved racism ideology have even found ways to defend the racial status quo by coining terms like "reverse racism" and demonizing anti-racist efforts like Diversity, Equity, and Inclusion, all consistent with the Anti-Woke campaigns used by white supremacists like Donald Trump and Ron DeSantis (Eibach & Keegan, 2006; Norton & Sommers, 2011). Many of the modern mechanisms that establish and perpetuate social inequality in American society remain invisible to the public (Bonilla-Silva, 2013). Thus, modern racist innuendos hide behind the guise of color blindness, a concept that critical race theorists argue against (Crenshaw, 2011).

Environmental Racism

The historical legacy of environmental racism can be traced back to these discriminatory practices of redlining, urban renewal projects, and the siting of hazardous facilities in predominantly Black neighborhoods. These practices have forced Black communities to bear the burden of pollution and environmental hazards while simultaneously facing limited access to green spaces, clean air, and clean water.

Environmental racism refers to the disproportionate exposure of marginalized communities, especially those belonging to minority groups, to environmental hazards and pollution. This occurs when companies and industries choose to locate hazardous facilities, such as waste disposal sites, factories, and power plants, in low-income neighborhoods and communities of color, exposing the residents to increased health risks and negative environmental impacts. This form of racism intersects with the broader framework of racial oppression and exacerbates existing social, economic, and health disparities.

Environmental racism is a manifestation of systemic racism that perpetuates environmental injustices and inequities. Communities of color, particularly Black communities, are often situated in close proximity to polluting industries, hazardous waste facilities, and degraded environments. These communities bear the brunt of harmful emissions, toxic pollutants, and environmental hazards, leading to adverse health outcomes and reduced quality of life.

Examining the examples of Black communities destroyed by highway construction, such as Overtown in Miami, Black Bottom in Detroit, West End in Cincinnati, Independence Heights in Houston, Tremé in New Orleans, and communities in Southern California, reveals the racially biased nature of urban planning. Racially restrictive covenants and discriminatory real estate practices further perpetuated segregation and limited Black communities' opportunities for growth and development. The role of the Home Owners' Loan Corporation (HOLC) in perpetuating racial inequality through redlining further exacerbated these disparities.

Some examples of environmental racism in the USA include:

Cop City in Atlanta, Georgia: In Atlanta, the development of the "Cop City" training center has sparked significant controversy, epitomizing the complex interplay between environmental justice, community engagement, and policing. Critics, dubbing the proposed $90 million facility "Cop City," oppose it on the grounds of environmental harm, as it threatens a substantial forest area and increased police militarization, which they argue endangers marginalized communities, particularly Black communities. This concern is heightened by the historical context of disproportionate policing and systemic injustices faced by Black residents, making the center a flashpoint for broader issues of racial equity and community autonomy. The tension escalated following the fatal shooting of a protester by police, leading to more protests and a state of emergency declaration. This conflict underscores the broader national discourse on balancing environmental preservation, community trust, and public safety in urban development, with a critical focus on the impacts on Black communities.

Flint, Michigan: In 2014, the city of Flint switched its water source to the Flint River, which was contaminated with lead and other toxins. This led to a public health crisis, and the majority of Flint's residents are African American. Despite its popularity, Flint is just one of the widespread environmental degradations that significantly impact Black Americans.

Cancer Alley, Louisiana: This stretch of the Mississippi River between Baton Rouge and New Orleans is home to more than 150 petrochemical plants and refineries. The predominantly African American and low-income communities living in the area are exposed to hazardous air and water pollution.

Navajo Nation, Arizona: The Navajo Nation, which is the largest Native American reservation in the US, has been negatively impacted by uranium mining and nuclear waste disposal. The Navajo people are exposed to radiation and other toxic substances, leading to high rates of cancer and other health issues.

West Oakland, California: This predominantly African American neighborhood is located near the Port of Oakland, which is a significant source of air pollution. The high levels of pollution from diesel trucks, cargo ships, and industrial facilities have contributed to respiratory problems, asthma, and other health issues among residents.

Standing Rock Sioux Tribe, North Dakota: The construction of the Dakota Access Pipeline (DAPL) through the Standing Rock Sioux Tribe's ancestral lands posed a significant threat to the tribe's water supply and sacred sites. The pipeline also puts neighboring communities at risk of oil spills and contamination. The Standing Rock Sioux Tribe, with the support of activists and environmental groups, led a resistance movement against the pipeline that garnered international attention.

Lowndes County, Alabama: This predominantly African American and low-income county has inadequate sewage infrastructure, which has led to a public health crisis. Many residents cannot afford to install septic systems and are forced to dispose of raw sewage in their yards, which has led to the spread of diseases such as hookworm.

East Chicago, Indiana: The West Calumet Housing Complex housed primarily African American and Latino families and was built on top of a former lead smelting plant. The soil and water in the area were contaminated with lead and other toxic substances, leading to elevated blood lead levels in children and other health problems.

Little Haiti Miami, Florida: Little Haiti in Miami exemplifies the intersection of environmental justice and racial equity in urban America. Predominantly inhabited by Haitian immigrants and their descendants, this community faces the dual challenges of gentrification and climate vulnerability. As developers encroach, rising property values threaten to displace long-term residents, undermining the area's rich cultural heritage and exacerbating economic disparities. Additionally, Little Haiti's susceptibility to climate change effects, such as rising sea levels and hurricanes, highlights the broader issue of environmental hazards disproportionately impacting minority communities. The struggles of Little Haiti resonate deeply within the discourse on American racism, illustrating how systemic inequalities often manifest in ecological and urban development contexts, significantly affecting Black communities and other marginalized groups.

The consequences of environmental racism are far-reaching. Studies have consistently shown that communities of color, particularly Black communities, experience higher rates of respiratory illnesses, including asthma, as well as higher cancer rates and other pollution-related health disparities. The correlation between exposure to pollution and a shorter lifespan is evident, with the impacts disproportionately affecting Black individuals.

Environmental racism exacerbates existing social and economic disparities within Black communities. Polluting industries and degraded environments hinder community development, economic growth, and educational opportunities. Moreover, the lack of access to healthy environments and green spaces deprives individuals and communities of the social, psychological, and physical benefits of a clean and sustainable environment.

The Effects of Racism on Black Communities

Racism has profound effects on individuals and communities, perpetuating social, economic, and health disparities. One significant impact of racism is the perpetuation of White privilege. White individuals disproportionately hold positions of power and influence in various domains, including education, politics, and business (Sue, 2003). This overrepresentation of Whites in influential positions creates an imbalance of power and perpetuates inequality.

Economically, racism results in significant wealth disparities. Research on economic equity have found that White households possess substantially greater wealth than Black and Hispanic households (Kochar, Fry, & Taylor, 2011). Structural racism, through historical discriminatory practices, limits access to wealth-building opportunities, contributing to wealth gaps between racial groups (Oliver & Shapiro, 2006). The consequences of this economic disparity are far-reaching, affecting education, housing, and overall socioeconomic well-being.

Health disparities are another significant effect of racism. Research has demonstrated a correlation between racism and adverse health outcomes, particularly for marginalized racial groups (Gee et al., 2012; Gee & Ford, 2011). Racism contributes to elevated rates of chronic diseases, such as hypertension, and increases the risk of mental health issues among racial minority populations (Brondolo et al., 2011; Pieterse et al., 2012). Racism also affects reproductive health, mortality rates, and access to quality healthcare (Collins & Williams, 1999; Mendez, Hogan, & Culhane, 2013).

Racism's impact extends to the psychological well-being of its victims. The experience of racism can lead to significant psychological distress, including race-based traumatic stress (Carter, 2007; Pieterse et al., 2012). Microaggressions, which are subtle and sometimes unintentional forms of racism, contribute to ongoing racial stress and feelings of marginalization (Sue et al., 2007). Moreover, racism can challenge the masculinity of Black males, leading to heightened aggression and illogical adherence to gender norms based on European cosmology (Goff, Di Leone, & Kahn, 2012).

Systemic Barriers and Challenges

Racism has far-reaching consequences that affect individuals and communities on multiple levels. One significant area impacted by racism is the economy, where racially based disparities persist (Bonilla-Silva, 2013; Gee, Ro, Shariff-Marco, & Chae, 2009; Jones, 2002). Due to discriminatory practices and systemic barriers, marginalized racial groups often face limited access to economic opportunities, lower wages, and reduced wealth accumulation. These economic disparities further perpetuate inequality and hinder social mobility.

Political consequences of racism are also evident, as it undermines equitable representation and the ability of marginalized communities to have their voices heard. Racist ideologies and discriminatory practices have historically marginalized non-White individuals in the political arena, leading to a lack of diverse perspectives and policies that address their specific needs and concerns.

Moreover, racism has profound social consequences. Studies have shown that social capital, which refers to the networks, relationships, and trust within a community, is highest in racially homogeneous White communities (Hero, 2007, Strouble 2015). This suggests that non-White communities, particularly African American communities, may face challenges in building, bridging, and linking social capital (Hobson-Prater & Leech, 2012; Patillio, 2005). Racism restricts the ability to establish meaningful connections across racial boundaries, resulting in reduced opportunities for collaboration, resource sharing, and social support.

Racism negatively affects the mental and physical health of individuals and communities. Research indicates that experiences of racial discrimination contribute to increased stress, anxiety, and adverse health outcomes among marginalized racial groups (Brondolo et al., 2012). The constant exposure to racism and its consequences takes a toll on the well-being of individuals, further exacerbating existing disparities in health outcomes.

The consequences of racism also extend to the educational realm, where racial disparities persist in access to quality education, educational resources, and academic achievement. Racist attitudes and systemic inequalities in educational institutions hinder the full potential and opportunities available to marginalized racial groups, perpetuating cycles of disadvantage and limiting their prospects.

It is essential to recognize that the consequences of racism are not borne solely by individuals from marginalized racial groups but impact society as a whole. When specific communities are held back due to racism, the entire society suffers from the loss of their contributions, talents, and perspectives.

Effects of Racial Oppression on Social Capital and Community Development

Racial oppression has significantly eroded social capital within Black communities. The erosion of trust and social cohesion has hindered community networks and support systems. Black communities have experienced a diminished sense of collective efficacy and empowerment, impeding their ability to address collective challenges and effect change. Furthermore, the intergenerational transmission of social capital has been disrupted, limiting the opportunities for upward mobility and community development.

In her seminal research article "Serial Forced Displacement and the Decline of Ubuntu in African American Communities" by Black Psychologist Huberta Jackson-Lowman (2020), the impact of serial forced displacement on Black communities in the United States is examined. Jackson-Lowman highlights how this ongoing Maafa or African Holocaust disrupts the concept of Ubuntu, which refers to the natural tendencies of respect, compassion, caring, cooperation, and support among individuals, all critical elements of social capital. Fullilove (2016), argues that racist displacement policies that disconnect people from their land, culture, history, traditions, values, and relationships creates "root shock" and undermines the manifestation of Ubuntu.

Both Jackson-Lowman and Fullilove assert that American housing policies, both at the federal and local levels, along with private development initiatives leading to gentrification, are major contributors to the decline of Ubuntu in Black communities. These policies result in the uprooting and destruction of thriving Black neighborhoods, causing community disorganization, health disparities, violence, and family instability, particularly in low-income areas. Moreover, the historical trajectory of housing policies in the United States, including segregation, redlining, and the Federal Housing Act of 1949 (Urban Renewal), has systematically dismantled African American neighborhoods and institutions, disproportionately affecting Black businesses and cultural networks, thereby severing the once strong connections within the Black community.

The economic disparities resulting from racial oppression have hindered wealth accumulation within Black communities. Limited access to resources and investment opportunities has further compounded the challenges faced by these communities. Moreover, the destruction of Black communities through highways and discriminatory urban planning practices, such as racially restrictive covenants and redlining, has had a lasting impact on community development and access to resources.

Racial oppression undermines social capital within Black communities, hindering their ability to mobilize resources, establish networks, and create sustainable change. Institutionalized racism limits access to education, employment, and other resources necessary for community development (Green, 2008; Vaught & Castagno, 2008). Personally mediated racism perpetuates social exclusion and hinders the formation of inclusive and cohesive communities (Pearson et al., 2009). Internalized racism sows self-doubt and diminishes community members' sense of collective empowerment (Pyke, 2010).

Figure 3: The Racial Oppression - Community Dysfunction Cycle

Understanding the Racism-Community Dysfunction Cycle

In this section, we delve into the interconnected relationship between racism and community dysfunction within the context of Black communities. By exploring the concept of the racism-community dysfunction cycle, we aim to shed light on how continuous experiences of racism contribute to social capital deficits and perpetuate harmful practices. This cycle reinforces barriers to social change, making it challenging for these communities to break free from the cycle of oppression (Strouble, 2015).

Racial Oppression

In the first stage of the cycle, ongoing systemic racism limits opportunities and resources available to Black communities, resulting in a significant disparity in access to political, economic, and social resources.

This inequity extends to public services, where Black communities often receive lower-quality education, healthcare, and infrastructure. Serial forced displacement continually uproots Black communities, disrupting their functionality. Racialized economic segregation further exacerbates these issues by enforcing economic policies and practices that result in economically and racially segregated communities, further limiting economic mobility and reinforcing poverty.

Social Capital Deficiencies

When Black communities operate under oppressive circumstances, they often are forced to develop despite severe social capital deficits. The networks, relationships, and resources that enable individuals and communities to navigate challenges and pursue collective goals are strained by internal and external factors manifested by historical and contemporary racist activity. The continuous experiences of racism erode the community's social trust. This, in turn, disrupts social cohesion and collaboration.

Community Cultural Dysfunctions

Social capital deficits within the community lead to the development of cultural dysfunctions. These dysfunctions are the result of communities being forced to adapt to the continuous problems and barriers created by racism. They can be understood as collective bad habits formed through traumatic experiences. The dysfunctions manifest in various ways, such as internalized oppression, distrust among community members, reduced civic engagement, and a lack of faith in collective efficacy. Persistent problems within the community remain unaddressed. Disillusionment with systems perpetuating injustice leads to contempt for political and legal systems, causing disengagement. The normalization of poverty affects community aspirations and behaviors, facilitating a culture of poverty. Furthermore, political isolation excludes community members from political processes and decision-making, while collective apathy results in a general lack of interest or concern about social issues. The ultimate consequence is reduced adaptive and transformative capacity, both necessities for preparing and responding to challenges and effecting positive change.

Barriers to Positive Social Change

As community cultural dysfunctions take hold, they reinforce existing barriers to social change. Economic stagnation, driven by systemic inequalities, hinders growth and development. Political corruption within governance systems further marginalizes the community and undermines reform efforts. Ineffective policy implementation means that policies designed to support the community are often poorly executed or inadequately enforced. The spread of misinformation and a lack of awareness about available resources and opportunities undermine community efforts. Inherited disadvantages, such as generational poverty and discrimination, create persistent barriers that are difficult to overcome. In addition, puppet leadership, where leaders prioritize personal or external interests over the community's needs, further undermines social trust and impedes collective progress. These barriers allow for continued racial oppression, thus completing the self-perpetuating cycle by increasing the difficulty for the community to break free from the grips of oppression. In Chapter 9, we will discuss strategies for breaking free from this cycle and fostering resilience and empowerment within Black communities.

Conclusion

This chapter has provided an in-depth exploration of racial oppression and its impact on Black communities. By adopting a critical race theory framework, we have gained insights into the multifaceted nature of racism and its different forms: institutionalized racism, personally mediated racism, and internalized racism. We have also examined the profound effects of racism, including social, economic, and health disparities. Recognizing the consequences of racism is crucial for promoting equity and social capital within Black communities and working toward dismantling systemic barriers.

To confront the realities of racism, the disparities that persist within our society must be acknowledged. People of color face disproportionate risks and burdens, including environmental pollution, healthcare disparities, biased criminal justice practices, and economic inequities. These systemic injustices create a cycle of inequality that impedes progress and hampers the full realization of human potential. Appropriate next steps and conversations should explore strategies and interventions to address racial oppression and foster community development that is inclusive, empowering, and transformative.

5

A Comprehensive Demographic Assessment of Contemporary Black America

"If there is no struggle, there is no progress."
Frederick Douglass

Establishing a baseline is an initial step to developing more effective plans for sustainability and resilience in Black American communities. Therefore, this chapter is dedicated to providing an overview of the current state of Black American communities by explicitly exploring residential and demographic trends. Throughout the chapter, I highlight key statistics and trends related to the population size, geographic distribution, migration patterns, educational attainment, and other pertinent social characteristics of Black Americans.

Population Growth

The U.S. Black population has grown consistently, reaching a record high of 47.2 million in 2021 (Moslimani et al., 2024). This growth is primarily attributed to changes in how race and ethnicity are calculated and the arrival of immigrants from Africa, the Caribbean, and other regions (Moslimani et al., 2024).

Regional Population Shifts

There is a growing trend of African Americans migrating back to the South (Sullivan, 2011). Several African Americans have been relocating to suburban neighborhoods in southern states due to institutional and market forces. Around 60% of the Black population now resides in ten states, with six of them located in the South. As recently as 2021, more than 50% of the Black population lived in the South.

Texas has the most Black residents, at 4 million, followed by Florida, with 3.8 million, and Georgia, with 3.6 million (Moslimani et al., 2024). The New York metropolitan area has the highest concentration of Black Americans, with nearly 4 million residing there. Other metro areas with substantial Black populations include Atlanta, Washington, D.C., and Chicago.

Residential Composition

Census tracts are geographic areas designated by the U.S. Census Bureau to represent communities and/or neighborhoods. These tracts usually have between 1,200 and 8,000 residents and average about 4,000. Planners and researchers often use census tracts to assess communities' or neighborhoods' unique characteristics. This level of microanalytic detail is exceptionally useful for making determinations that affect the lives of people who live in those neighborhoods.

According to the U.S. Census Bureau (2022), there were 85,396 Census Tracts in 2022. Recently, 8,766, or 10.2%, of these tracts are reportedly majority Black, a slight decrease in proportion from 11.2% (7,258 tracts) in 2010. Furthermore, much of America's Black population is spread across 76,067 census tracts, with nearly 47% living in majority Black tracts where they are the predominant racial group (U.S. Census Bureau, 2022). Additionally, 20% of Black Americans live in approximately 3,000 "low-diversity tracts" (more than 75% Black). Another 23% reside in about 4,500 tracts considered moderately diverse, with Black residents making up 50-74% (U.S. Census Bureau, 2022). This data reflects a trend towards greater diversity, with fewer low-diversity tracts and more with diverse populations.

In 2000, 50% of the African Americans resided in metropolitan areas. (Patillo, 2005). Over time, the proportion declined, from 70.3% in 1960 to 56.2% in 1990, reaching 50.4% in 2000 (Patillo, 2005). In the same year, about 30% of African Americans lived in communities that were at least 80% Black, with 87% of them residing in non-poor neighborhoods (Patillo, 2005).

Despite decreases in residential segregation, several challenges stemming from persistent racial inequality and poverty continue to plague Black communities. While African Americans have seen limited progress in accessing neighborhoods with resources equivalent to those of Whites and Asians at similar income levels, segregation has lessened. Yet still, Black Americans often remain economically isolated and are more likely to inhabit areas with higher poverty rates and more significant environmental risks.

Pollution and Climate Exposure

Studies have consistently shown that Black Americans are disproportionately exposed to environmental hazards when compared to their White counterparts. Jbaily et al. (2022) found that Black Americans experienced an average PM2.5 concentration that was 13.7% higher than White Americans and 36.3% higher than Native Americans. This disparity is not confined to specific income levels or regions and has worsened over time (Jbaily et al., 2022). Additionally, Black Americans are more likely to reside near highways and major roads, which are significant sources of nitrogen dioxide emissions from transportation. Approximately 78% of African Americans live within 30 miles of a coal-fired power plant, exposing them to higher levels of toxic emissions (Climate Reality Project, 2023). Diesel emissions further exacerbate health risks in Black communities. National statistics project that diesel pollution is likely to result in approximately 8,822 deaths, 3,728 heart attacks, and 105,947 cases of asthma annually as of 2023. The economic burden of diesel-related health damages is nearly $98 billion annually (Climate Reality Project, 2023).

Climate change poses additional risks to Black communities. Extreme weather events, including but not limited to wildfires, heatwaves, hurricanes, and flooding, are becoming more frequent and intense. Black populations, particularly in the Southeast United States, are disproportionately affected by these climate hazards (McKinsey & Company, 2023). For instance, Black communities, for example, are 1.4 times more likely to be exposed to extreme heat and 1.8 times more likely to experience hurricanes than the overall U.S. population in the same regions (McKinsey & Company, 2023). By 2050, nearly one in seven Black-owned homes will be at risk of storm damage, with 12.6% exposed to severe flooding (McKinsey & Company, 2023).

The residual impacts of historical redlining and contemporary environmental racism leave Black neighborhoods exceptionally vulnerable. Previously redlined areas often lack green spaces and adequate tree canopy. As a result, they are inundated with asphalt and concrete, causing them to experience urban heat island effects, higher temperatures, and increased flood risks.

The energy burden is another strenuous concern in Black communities, and it underscores the profound disparities in energy consumption and its consequences on Black Americans' economic well-being. Recent research has unveiled a troubling pattern. Neighborhoods with the lowest incomes and a higher proportion of non-white residents consume more energy (Tong et al., 2021). These communities, already grappling with economic challenges, use significantly more energy for heating and cooling than their more affluent and racially diverse counterparts (Tong et al., 2021). The stark disparities persist even after accounting for income levels, revealing a complex interplay of factors (Tong et al., 2021). Building age, education levels, family size, and the presence of trees in an area all contribute to these disparities (Tong et al., 2021). Addressing the energy burden is not merely an environmental concern but a critical component in the broader struggle for economic justice and equity within Black communities.

Education Trends

An examination of Black education indicators reveals some areas of progress along with lingering disparities in access and outcomes. Contemporary policies seem to exacerbate historic challenges, furthering the struggles of African American students.

Early Childhood Education

As of 2022, early childhood education enrollment rates for Black children between 3 and 4 were 48%, compared to 50% for White children and slightly lower than the rate for Asian children at 52%, while the overall national average was approximately 45% (US Department of Education, 2024).

For 5-year-olds, the overall school enrollment rate for Black children was 85%, closely aligned with the rates for Asian children at 86% and White children at 84%, while the national average for this age group was around 84%. These statistics indicate that Black children generally keep pace with their peers in early childhood education enrollment (US Department of Education, 2024).

However, the data indicated that Black children rely more on public schooling for early education compared to their peers from other racial and ethnic backgrounds. These trends highlight ongoing disparities and preferences in early childhood education within the Black community, emphasizing a significant reliance on public education over private schooling options.

Enrollment Patterns

During the 2009-2010 school year, 8,166,353 Black children attended public schools and 430,972 in private schools. Notably, more African American children were enrolled in charter schools (488,233) than in private schools, indicating a growing presence of African American students in the charter school movement.

Private Schools: Private schools are a significant educational option for many African American students, especially those in religious settings. As of fall 2021, about 4.7 million K-12 students (constituting 9% of the combined public and private school population) were enrolled in private schools (National Center for Education Statistics, 2024). Among African American private school students, 75% are in religious schools, with 35% attending Catholic schools. This trend can be attributed to the affordability and accessibility of Catholic schools, even though only 5% of African Americans identify as Catholic. The remaining 18% of these students are distributed among other religious denominations, including non-conservative Christian groups, Jewish, Islamic, and other faiths (National Center for Education Statistics, 2024).

Concerning demographics, private school students differ notably from their public school counterparts. In fall 2021, 65% of private school students were White compared to 45% in public schools. Additionally, 9% of private school students were Black, compared to 15% in public schools (National Center for Education Statistics, 2024). This disparity extends to poverty rates, with 11% of private school students living in poverty versus 17% of public school students (National Center for Education Statistics, 2024).

Voucher programs, which allocate public funds to support private school tuition, disproportionately benefit non-Black students while creating significant financial challenges for Black communities. Given the limited capacity of Black private schools and the low overall enrollment of Black students in private institutions, these programs divert essential resources away from public schools, which serve the vast majority of Black children. This practice effectively dispossesses Black students of the funding needed to address inequities in their education, channeling public dollars into private institutions that predominantly serve White and non-Black students.

These trends indicate that while private schools accommodate a significant number of African American students, the distribution and demographic characteristics of these students reveal ongoing disparities and preferences within the educational system.

Charter Schools: Charter schools have experienced significant growth nationwide, contributing significantly to the education of African American students. Between the 1999-2000 and 2009-2010 school years, enrollment of African American students in charter schools surged from 113,792 to 488,233. This trend has continued over the years, reflecting a broader demographic shift in charter schools.

From fall 2010 to fall 2021, the racial composition of public charter schools saw notable changes. The percentage of Hispanic students in charter schools increased from 27% to 36%, and students of two or more races rose from 3% to 5%. Conversely, the percentage of White students decreased from 36% to 29%, and Black students from 29% to 24% (National Center for Education Statistics, 2024). This decrease in

Black student enrollment in charter schools mirrors a broader national trend seen across public schools.

In terms of socioeconomic demographics, a higher percentage of charter school students attended high-poverty schools compared to their counterparts in traditional public schools. As of fall 2021, 31% of charter school students were in schools where over 75% of their peers were eligible for free or reduced-price lunch (FRPL), compared to 21% of traditional public school students. Conversely, fewer charter school students attended low-poverty schools (17%) compared to conventional public school students (25%) (National Center for Education Statistics, 2024).

These data highlight the dynamic changes in charter school enrollment and underscore the significant role these schools play in the education of African American students. The trends also suggest ongoing challenges related to racial composition and socioeconomic status within the charter school system.

Homeschool: Homeschooling has increased overall in the United States over the past two decades. In 2019, 2.8% (1,457,000) of students ages 5 to 17 were homeschooled, compared to 1.7% (850,000) in 1999. However, the percentage of homeschooled students was slightly lower in 2019 than the peak of 3.4% in 2012 (National Center for Education Statistics, 2020).

Among Black students, the homeschooling rate in 2019 was 1.2%, which is lower compared to other racial/ethnic groups. For instance, 4.0% of White students and 2.7% of students of two or more races were homeschooled (National Center for Education Statistics, 2020). This indicates that while homeschooling is an educational choice for some Black families, it is less prevalent compared to other demographics

Graduation and Dropout Rates

Graduation rates for African American students have significantly improved, though disparities with the national average persist. The four-year graduation rate for Black students currently stands at 63.6%, compared to the national rate of 80.6%. Notably, the dropout rate for African American students is lower than the national average, with only 8% of Black students dropping out of high school in 2010, compared to 7.4% for all students. The dropout rate for Black students fell dramatically from 33% in 1968 to 5% in 2018, aligning closely with the national average of 6% (Cheeseman Day, 2020). This represents a significant decline from the dropout rates of 21.3% in 1972 and 13.1% in 2000.

Recent U.S. Census data further highlights this progress. As of 2020, 88% of Black Americans have completed high school, just slightly below the national average of 90% (Cheeseman Day, 2020). This is an extremely remarkable achievement and a testament to the power of Black education initiatives, especially considering that in 1940, only 7% of Black Americans had a high school education, compared to 24% of the nation as a whole (Cheeseman Day, 2020).

African American high school seniors increasingly plan to attend colleges and universities and pursue graduate or professional education. The percentage of Black seniors with definite plans to attend a four-year college doubled between 1990 and 2010, rising from 30% to 60%. However, there has been only a slight increase in plans to attend a two-year college, from 16% to 19%.

Academic Achievement Gap

Despite efforts to narrow the Black-White achievement gap, significant disparities persist. Data from the National Assessment of Educational Progress (NAEP) indicates that from 1990 to 2011, the achievement gap in 8th-grade mathematics scores decreased by 7 points. In 8th grade, reading scores decreased from 32 points to 24 points between 1992 and 2009. However, much work remains to ensure equitable academic outcomes for Black students. For instance, 2020 NAEP data showed that lower-performing students (10th percentile) in reading and mathematics scored lower than in 2012. In mathematics, scores for 9-year-olds at the 10th and 25th percentiles and 13-year-olds at the

10th, 25th, and 50th percentiles were all lower in 2020 compared to 2012 (National Center for Education Statistics, 2022).

Progress toward closing achievement gaps is evident, yet disparities remain substantial. For instance, in reading, the White-Black and White-Hispanic score gaps for ages 9 and 13 were smaller in 2020 compared to the 1970s (National Center for Education Statistics, 2022). The average reading score for White 13-year-olds increased by 8 points from 1971 to 2020, while Black 13-year-olds saw a 22-point gain, reducing the gap from 39 points in 1971 to 24 points in 2020 (National Center for Education Statistics, 2022). In mathematics, the White-Black gap for 13-year-olds narrowed by 7 points from 1978 to 2020 due to a 27-point increase in Black students' scores compared to a 19-point increase for White students (National Center for Education Statistics, 2022). However, between 2012 and 2020, Black 13-year-olds' mathematics scores declined by 8 points, widening the gap by 6 points (National Center for Education Statistics, 2022).

Teacher Disparities

According to the National Center for Education Statistics (2017), most Black public schools face significant challenges in attracting and retaining certified teachers with degrees in their teaching subjects. For instance, a lower percentage of math teachers in majority Black schools have math as their major in college compared to non-Black public schools (National Center for Education Statistics, 2017). Similar disparities exist in the qualifications of English and science teachers. Moreover, Black teachers may have more positive expectations for Black students' achievement than non-Black teachers (National Center for Education Statistics, 2017).

The racial/ethnic composition of public elementary and secondary school teachers shows a majority of White teachers. In 2003–04, 83% of teachers were White, which decreased slightly to 80% by 2015–16. The percentage of Black teachers also reduced from 8% in 2003–04 to 7% in 2015–16. Conversely, the percentages of Hispanics, Asians, and teachers of Two or more races increased during the same period. Schools with more racial/ethnic diversity in their student populations also tended to have more racial/ethnic diversity among teachers. For example, at schools with 90% or more minority students, 55% of teachers were minorities. In contrast, at schools with less than 10% minority students, 98% of the teachers were White (National Center for Education Statistics, 2017).

These disparities highlight the need for targeted efforts to improve the recruitment and retention of qualified minority teachers in majority Black schools to foster a more inclusive and supportive educational environment.

Higher Education

Higher Educational attainment among Black Americans has been on the rise. In 2021, 26% of Black adults aged 25 and older had earned a bachelor's degree or higher, up from 15% in 2000 (Pew Research Center, 2023). Both Black women and men have seen an increase in educational attainment, but the gender gap has widened, with 29% of Black women having earned at least a bachelor's degree compared to 22% of Black men in 2021.

The establishment of the first HBCU in the 1830s, prior to the Civil War, played a crucial role in providing Black Americans with opportunities for higher education. After years of decline, a number of historically Black colleges and universities (HBCUs) are experiencing an increase in Black student applications and enrollments. HBCUs like Morehouse College in Atlanta, Georgia, and Florida A&M University in Tallahassee have witnessed a surge in applications, with a remarkable increase of over 60% in 2020 compared to the previous year, as reported by Data USA.

There are currently 101 accredited HBCUs educating about 300,000 of America's 21 million college students. According to the United Negro College Fund, currently, 25% of Black graduates with STEM degrees come from HBCUs (Murray, Njoku and Davis, 2022). According to the National Center for Education Statistics, the percentage of Black students enrolled at HBCUs fell from 18% in 1976 to 8% in 2014 but has since risen to 9% in 2020. At its height, there were 136 HBCUs.

However, HBCUs face challenges such as financial difficulties and ongoing debates regarding the necessity of affirmative action policies. Additionally, the COVID-19 pandemic has impacted Black student enrollment in higher education overall, as noted by an analysis from the Latino Policy and Politics Institute at the University of California, Los Angeles, which focused on the pandemic's influence on enrollment among students of color.

Economic Status

Despite an increase in median income for African Americans since the Great Recession of 2008, the racial income gap persists. African Americans were the last major racial/ethnic group to begin recovering from the recession. As of 2022, Black households had a median annual income of $50,000, with multiracial Black households earning $60,000, Black Hispanic households earning $56,500, and single-race Black households earning $49,500. About half of all Black households (51%) had an income of $50,000 or more, while 49% earned less. Black men with a bachelor's degree earn only 77 cents for every dollar that all American men with a bachelor's degree earn, while Black women with a bachelor's degree earn 85 cents for every dollar that all American women with a bachelor's degree earn (Blackdemographics.com, 2023; ACS 2022 1-Year estimates).

Historically, African American incomes grew significantly during the 1990s. By 2000, about 44% of African American households had an annual income of $50,000 or more, compared to just 22% in 1969. However, the Great Recession significantly impacted these gains, reducing the percentage of Black households earning $50,000 or more to 38% by 2010. The most dramatic change was the increase in Black households making under $15,000, which rose from 18% in 2000 to 22% in 2012. Although the economic rebound was slowest for the Black population, by 2018, Black median incomes grew closer to recovery, and the Black upper class and wealthy grew to its most significant percentage ever.

Despite these improvements, Black median incomes remain significantly lower than the national average. For example, the median income for Black families is $28,000 less than the national family median income. This disparity is also evident when comparing Black married-couple families to female householder families, with the former making more than twice the income of the latter.

Recent data highlights that Black households made gains in terms of wealth during the pandemic. The typical single-race, non-Hispanic Black household saw a 77% increase in its wealth from December 2019 ($15,300) to December 2021 ($27,100) (Lopez & Moslimani, 2024). These gains, however, must be viewed within the broader context of persistent wealth gaps and economic disparities.

Predictive models indicate that the racial wealth gap will likely continue to widen, with the median Black household wealth projected to reach zero by 2082, followed by median Latino household wealth twenty years later (Collins et al., 2019). In stark contrast, median White household wealth is expected to grow to $137,000 by 2053 (Collins et al., 2017). Recent trends show that since 2020, median Black and Latino households have experienced significant wealth losses of approximately 18% and 12%, respectively, compared to their 2013 levels. Meanwhile, median White household wealth is expected to increase by 3%, leading to White households possessing 86 times more wealth than Black households and 68 times more wealth than Latino households by that point (Collins et al., 2019).

Black Businesses

In 2021, Black-owned businesses in the U.S. experienced significant growth, with the number of firms increasing from 124,004 in 2017 to 161,031 (Leppart, 2023). Despite this progress, Black-owned businesses still comprise a small share of all U.S. firms, making up only 3% of classifiable firms and accounting for just 1% of gross revenue (Leppart,

2023). The health care and social assistance sector is the most common industry for Black-owned businesses, followed by professional, scientific, and technical services (Leppart, 2023). Most Black-owned firms are small, with two-thirds having fewer than ten employees. Most of these businesses are located in urban areas, with Florida, California, and Georgia having the highest numbers. Black business owners are more likely to be men, middle-aged, and possess a college degree (Leppart, 2023). Their motivations often include the opportunity for more significant income, the desire to be their own boss, and the need for flexible working hours (Leppart, 2023).

Black Employment

In March 2023, the Black unemployment rate reached a record low of 5%. Although this rate remains 1.5% higher than the overall American unemployment rate, it represents a substantial reduction in the employment gap that has persisted for many years (BlackDemographics.com, 2023). Historically, Black unemployment rates have often doubled the overall rate, but recent trends indicate a significant narrowing of this gap. This improvement is accompanied by a rise in labor force participation among African Americans, which now surpasses that of the general American population, suggesting that more African Americans are actively seeking and obtaining employment opportunities. However, this should be cautioned with the rise of the "gig economy," which may distort unemployment figures by removing those temporarily employed from the count.

Bureau of Labor Statistics (2024) data reveals that the Black unemployment rate stood at 13% in 2013 during the recovery from the 2008 Great Recession. This rate steadily declined over the years, reaching a historic low of 5.3% in 2019. However, the COVID-19 pandemic caused a dramatic spike, with the rate surging to 18.8% in 2020. The unemployment rate began to decline again in the latter part of the Trump administration. It continued under the Biden administration, reaching the unprecedented low of 5.0% in March 2023 (Bureau of

Labor Statistics, 2024). Contributing factors include the widespread adoption of remote work, recovery of pandemic-affected industries, and financial pressures from inflation and housing costs.

While the decline in the Black unemployment rate is a positive development, challenges remain regarding job quality and wage disparities. African American workers continue to face barriers in accessing higher-paying and more secure employment, including occupational segregation and discriminatory hiring practices. Limited career advancement opportunities further contribute to these disparities.

Black Public Health

In addition to the socioeconomic factors discussed earlier, Black Americans face significant challenges related to racism and discrimination, which have profound effects on their public health outcomes (Brondolo et al., 2012). Ongoing exposure to stressors associated with racism and discrimination leads to poorer health outcomes among Black individuals (Brondolo et al., 2012). Health disparities continue to affect Black communities, with access to healthcare and life expectancy being critical areas of concern.

The state of health in Black America is influenced by various factors, including limited access to appropriate healthcare and high rates of obesity, cancer, and other chronic and fatal illnesses (Brondolo et al., 2012). African Americans face barriers to receiving preventative care, leading to higher susceptibility and mortality rates for diseases (Ndugga & Artiga, 2023). Even when the incidence rate of a particular disease is lower for African Americans, their death rates are often higher due to inadequate healthcare access (Ndugga & Artiga, 2023). Notably, the life expectancy for Black men is particularly concerning, with many unlikely to live past 70 years of age and experiencing challenges in accessing retirement benefits such as social security (Johnson et al., 2022; Ndugga & Artiga, 2023). Environmental factors also impact the health of Black males, contributing to higher rates of homicides and the recent surge in HIV infections (Ndugga & Artiga, 2023).

Food Insecurity and Nutrition Challenges

Food insecurity and poor nutrition are critical public health issues disproportionately affecting Black communities. Roughly 1 in 5 African American families live in food deserts, areas with limited access to affordable and nutritious food (Mickensey & Company, 2021). This lack of access leads to diets high in processed foods and low in essential nutrients, contributing to higher rates of obesity, diabetes, and other diet-related illnesses.

Historical erasure of Black farmers, who are few in number, also face significant challenges from climate change, which affects their crop yields and economic stability. As of 2017, Black people owned just 2 percent of farmland in the United States, primarily due to a long history of loan denials by the USDA (Holloway, 2021). There is reasonable speculation that a correlation exists between dwindling inclusion in farming and increasing food insecurity in Black American communities.

Access to Health Care

Disparities in health insurance coverage persist among African Americans. The National Health Interview Survey (2016) revealed that 11.6% of Black individuals under the age of 65 did not have health insurance, compared to 1.2% of those over 65. Limited access to healthcare, including preventative care for both children and adults, contributes to higher susceptibility to diseases and illnesses within the Black community.

Life Expectancy

While life expectancy has increased for all Americans over the last century, African Americans still experience a lower life expectancy than

Whites (Johnson et al., 2022). However, the gap has narrowed over time (Johnson et al., 2022). In 1900, there was a 14-year difference in life expectancy between Black and White individuals, which decreased to four years by 2010 (Johnson et al., 2022). Unfortunately, since 2014, life expectancy rates for both Black and White Americans have been decreasing, with factors such as the opioid epidemic contributing to this decline (Johnson et al., 2022).

Mental Health

While overall rates of mental illness and substance use disorders are lower for Black people compared to White people, there may be under-diagnosis among people of color. However, data suggest that mental health needs are on the rise among the Black population (Panchal, Saunders, & Ndugga, 2022). Black people have experienced a faster increase in deaths by suicide and drug overdose deaths compared to their White counterparts (Panchal, Saunders, & Ndugga, 2022). These findings underscore the importance of addressing mental health needs among the Black population and reducing barriers to treatment.

Additionally, people of color face disproportionate barriers to accessing mental health care. These barriers include lack of health insurance coverage, financial and logistical challenges, and the absence of a diverse mental health care workforce. The American Psychological Association's Center for Workforce Studies indicates that while Hispanic and Black people account for 30% of the U.S. population, they only represent 9% of the psychology workforce. This lack of representation can hinder treatment access and retention, as racial/ethnic concordance between patients and providers significantly impacts patients' experiences with their care providers. Furthermore, stigma associated with mental illness can deter Black adults from seeking mental health care, as mental health conditions may be perceived as signs of personal weakness, leading to concerns about discrimination and shame (Panchal, Saunders, & Ndugga, 2022).

Crime and Violence

Crime in Black America is a complex issue with significant implications for individuals and communities. A recent analysis of federal data highlights concerning trends in gun-related deaths and homicides among Black individuals (Rees et al., 2022). In 2021, the rate of gun deaths in the U.S. reached a 28-year high, driven by sharp increases in homicides of Black men and suicides among White men (Rees et al., 2022). Rees et al. (2022) reported a record 48,953 gun-related deaths in the U.S., equivalent to about 15 fatalities per 100,000 people. This marks a significant increase from the decline in gun deaths experienced in the 1990s, with a steady rise over the past decade and a drastic surge during the COVID-19 pandemic (Rees et al., 2022).

The Violence Policy Center (2023) found further insight into the homicide rates among Black victims in the United States. In 2016, there were 7,756 Black homicide victims, with a homicide rate of 20.44 per 100,000 (Violence Policy Center, 2023). Comparatively, the overall national homicide rate was 5.10 per 100,000, and for Whites, it was 2.96 per 100,000. Of the Black homicide victims, 87% were male, 13% were female, and a small percentage were of unknown sex (Violence Policy Center, 2023). The homicide rate for Black male victims was 37.12 per 100,000, significantly higher than the overall rate for male victims (8.29 per 100,000) and white male victims (4.39 per 100,000) (Violence Policy Center, 2023). The homicide rate for Black female victims was 5.07 per 100,000, compared to 1.97 per 100,000 for female victims overall and 1.55 per 100,000 for white female victims (Violence Policy Center, 2023).

Examining the circumstances of homicides where information was available, a considerable portion (71%) of cases were unrelated to the commission of any other felony (Rees et al., 2022). Among these cases, 48% involved arguments between the victim and the offender, while 17% were reported to be gang-related (Rees et al., 2022). The data also reveals 116 incidents reported as justifiable homicides of Black victims killed by law enforcement in 2016 (Rees et al., 2022). However, it is essential to note that the data does not explicitly identify killings by law enforcement that are not ruled justifiable, highlighting the need for more reliable statistics in this area. Efforts have been made to improve data collection on lethal incidents involving law enforcement (Rees et al., 2022).

State rankings further demonstrate the disproportionate impact of homicides on the Black community. In 2016, the national black homicide victimization rate stood at 20.44 per 100,000 (Violence Policy Center, 2023). Missouri ranked as the state with the highest black homicide victimization rate, with a rate of 46.21 per 100,000, more than double the national average for black homicide victimization (Violence Policy Center, 2023).

In 2020, the death rate for Black women saw a notable increase amid rising homicides and the impact of the COVID-19 pandemic (Violence Policy Center, 2023). As homicides increased nearly 30% nationwide, the rate for Black women and girls rose by 33%, surpassing the increase observed in every demographic except Black men and more than double the increase for White women (Violence Policy Center, 2023). Gun violence played a significant role, with three-quarters of homicide victims who were Black women and girls dying from gunshot wounds (Rees et al., 2022). This exacerbates an ongoing crisis of violence against Black women, which has been largely overlooked by various institutions and organizations (Violence Policy Center, 2023). Advocates highlight the silence surrounding this issue, despite Black women being expected to care for others but often not receiving the same level of care in return.

Available data indicates that, similar to most American women, Black women are often killed by someone they know (Rees et al., 2022). Law enforcement homicide data reported to the FBI shows that nearly a third of Black women and girls in 2020 were known to be killed by an intimate partner or a family member, while another 16% were killed by a friend, neighbor, or acquaintance (Rees et al., 2022). Racial segregation in neighborhoods and schools contributes to the fact that many homicide victims are killed by someone of the same race, typically a man, according to FBI national homicide statistics.

Police violence against and killings of Black people have become a distressing issue. Black people are more than three times as likely to be killed by police than White people, with approximately 1 in every 1,000 Black men expected to be killed by the police over their lifetime (Asabor et al., 2023). This repeated exposure to police violence has detrimental effects on the mental health of Black individuals (Asabor et al., 2023).

Furthermore, gun violence disproportionately affects Black communities, especially Black youth. The adverse impact of gun violence on the mental health and well-being of children is significant. Data indicate that firearm death rates among Black youth sharply increased during the pandemic, primarily due to gun assaults and suicides by firearm (Rees et al., 2022).

Family Structure

According to the March 2020 Current Population Survey, 37% of Black children live in homes headed by their own two biological parents, 48% live in single-parent homes, and 4% live in stepfamilies with one biological parent and one non-biological parent. Black children in single-parent homes are approximately 3.5 times more likely to experience poverty compared to those living with two parents in intact marriages. The likelihood of poverty is about 2.5 times higher for Black children in likely stepfamilies. Controlling for factors such as maternal education, age, children's age, and gender, the odds of poverty are 3.7 times higher for Black children in non-intact families compared to those in intact, married families. Statistically, it is clear that Black children in stable, married families have better financial circumstances.

Data from the National Longitudinal Survey of Youth (NLSY97) highlights significant disparities in educational outcomes based on family structure among Black young adults. Those raised in intact families with married biological parents are nearly twice as likely to graduate from college compared to those from single-parent families and approximately 1.5 times more likely than those from stepfamilies (Wilcox, Wang, & Rowe, 2021). After controlling for variables such as maternal education, gender, age, and Armed Forces Qualification Test scores, the likelihood of Black young adults obtaining a college degree increases by about 70% if both biological parents raised them. This suggests that, on average, Black young adults from two-parent households are more likely to achieve educational success compared to their peers from non-intact families (Wilcox, Wang, & Rowe, 2021).

Family structure also correlates strongly with incarceration rates among Black young adults. Those from single-parent homes are approximately 1.8 times more likely to have been incarcerated by their late twenties compared to those from intact families (Wilcox, Wang, & Rowe, 2021). Similarly, Black young adults from stepfamilies also face higher incarceration rates. Controlling for the same factors, the odds of incarceration for those from non-intact families are nearly double those from intact families (Wilcox, Wang, & Rowe, 2021).

When disaggregating data by gender, similar patterns emerge. Black men from intact, two-parent families are significantly more likely to graduate from college and have lower incarceration rates compared to their peers from single-parent or stepfamilies (Wilcox, Wang, & Rowe, 2021). For Black women, more than one-third of those from intact families attain a college degree by their late twenties, while the rates are 18% and 25% for those from single-parent and stepfamilies, respectively (Wilcox, Wang, & Rowe, 2021).

Comparing these patterns with White children reveals further insights. According to the March 2020 Current Population Survey, 67% of white children live in homes headed by their biological parents, while 21% live in single-parent homes and 6% with a biological parent and stepparent (CPS, 2020). Black children from intact families generally fare better than white children from single-parent households across various outcomes such as poverty, college graduation, and incarceration. For instance, 36% of young Black women from intact families graduate from college, compared to 28% of young White women from single-parent families (Wilcox, Wang, & Rowe, 2021). Additionally, the incarceration rate for young Black men from intact families is 14%, compared to 24% for those from single-parent families and 26% for those from stepfamilies (Wilcox, Wang, & Rowe, 2021). Poverty rates also reflect this trend: 13% of Black children in intact families experience poverty, while 33% of White children in single-parent families do (Wilcox, Wang, & Rowe, 2021).

Despite these findings, within each family structure category, White young adults generally have more advantages. For example, 47% of White young adults from intact families have graduated from college, compared to 28% of Black young adults from intact families (Wilcox, Wang, & Rowe, 2021). This highlights that stable, two-parent families are not a panacea for addressing racial inequalities. Structural factors such as historical racial discrimination, unequal access to quality education, and ongoing experiences of racial prejudice contribute significantly to these disparities.

The association between family structure and child outcomes in terms of poverty and incarceration is similar for Black and White children. Regardless of race, growing up in non-intact homes more than triples the odds of experiencing poverty and doubles the odds of incarceration (Wilcox, Wang, & Rowe, 2021). However, the link between family structure and college graduation is less pronounced for Black children compared to White children. Controlling for relevant factors, growing up in a non-intact family reduces the odds of college graduation by 60% for white young adults but only by 40% for Black young adults (Wilcox, Wang, & Rowe, 2021). Nevertheless, young adults from intact families, whether Black or White, are significantly more likely to graduate from college than their peers from non-intact families.

This analysis underscores that both Black and White children raised in intact homes are significantly more likely to avoid poverty, attain higher education, and avoid incarceration. However, racial inequalities persist, even within the same family structure. Black children in stable, two-parent families are more likely to face poverty and incarceration and less likely to graduate from college compared to their white peers from similar family structures. This suggests that while family structure plays a crucial role in child outcomes, addressing broader structural inequities is essential for achieving true racial equality.

It is crucial to note that this descriptive research brief does not establish causality, as various unmeasured factors may influence the associations between family structure and child outcomes. Factors such as family income, which is influenced by family structure, and other structural elements like access to quality education, concentrated poverty, and experiences of racial prejudice are essential considerations in understanding the racial differences observed in outcomes between children from different family structures. Nonetheless, it remains evident that, in line with the longstanding social scientific consensus, children are significantly more likely to avoid poverty and prison and to graduate from college when raised in intact, two-parent families. This holds true for both Black and white children, with the vast majority of such families being headed by the children's married biological parents.

Religion and Culture

Black American religious practices have been a significant part of the community's identity and experience. According to a Pew Research Center (2021) survey, prayer plays a central role in the lives of most Black adults when making major decisions, and opposing racism is seen as essential to their religious faith. Furthermore, predominantly Black places of worship continue to hold a strong presence in the lives of Black Americans, with 60% of Black adults who attend religious services reporting that they do so at predominantly Black congregations (Pew Research Center, 2021).

However, there are indications that these patterns are evolving, particularly among younger generations. The survey reveals that Black Millennials and Generation Z individuals are less religious and less engaged in Black churches compared to older generations. They rely less on prayer, are less likely to have grown up in Black churches, and consider religion to be less important in their lives (Pew Research Center, 2021). Additionally, fewer young Black adults attend religious services, and those who do attend are less likely to be part of predominantly Black congregations (Pew Research Center, 2021).

Historically, Protestantism has been the dominant religious affiliation among Black Americans, and it remains so today, with 66% identifying as Protestant. Another 6% identify as Catholic, 3% as followers of other Christian faiths (mainly Jehovah's Witnesses), and 3% as belonging to non-Christian faiths, with Islam being the most common (Pew Research Center, 2021).

However, the survey also highlights a growing trend of religious disaffiliation, with 21% of Black Americans identifying as atheist, agnostic, or having no particular religious affiliation (Pew Research Center, 2021). This trend is particularly prominent among younger generations, with 28% of Black "Gen Zers" and 33% of Black Millennials being religiously unaffiliated.

Comparing the religious commitment of Black Americans with the general population, the survey finds that Black Americans are generally more religious (Pew Research Center, 2021). They are more likely to believe in God or a higher power, attend religious services regularly, consider religion vital in their lives, and be affiliated with a religious denomination (Pew Research Center, 2021). Moreover, their perspectives on religion and religious groups differ from those of the general population. Black Americans are more likely to view opposition to racism as essential to religious faith. They are more likely to credit predominantly Black Muslim organizations, such as the Nation of Islam, for their role in advancing equality for Black people in the United States (Pew Research Center, 2021).

These findings highlight the evolving landscape of Black American religious practices, with generational shifts and changing patterns of affiliation and engagement. Understanding these dynamics is crucial for comprehensively understanding the Black community's diverse religious experiences and perspectives.

Political Status

Black Americans have made significant strides in U.S. political leadership, yet disparities and gaps remain in some regions of representation. The election of Kamala Harris as the first Black woman vice president marked a historic moment, highlighting the progress made by Black Americans in recent decades. This section examines the representation of Black Americans in various political positions, acknowledging both the advancements achieved and the challenges that persist.

Black Partisan Affiliation

Contemporary Black partisan affiliation remains remarkably one-sided in favor of the Democratic Party, even as we approach six decades since the Civil Rights movement. Overall, 87% of black voters identify with the Democratic Party or lean Democratic, compared with just 7% who identify as Republican or lean Republican. Researchers exploring the factors behind this enduring trend have found that generational differences and regional factors contribute to some variation in political allegiance among African Americans (PEW Research Center, 2016). Generational shifts have led younger cohorts to exhibit a slightly higher Republican party identification than those who lived through the Civil Rights era. However, voting patterns established during the Civil Rights movement continue to shape Black partisan identification today (King, 2006). Furthermore, perceived hostility from the Republican party still serves to dissuade Black Voters from considering bipartisan political approaches.

Political Representation

The progress made by Black Americans in political leadership is evident, particularly in the House of Representatives and particular presidential Cabinets. However, challenges persist in achieving equitable representation in the Senate and governorships. Efforts should continue to focus on increasing the presence of Black Americans in these positions, as more excellent political representation has the potential to contribute to increased racial equality and address systemic disparities. By actively working towards diverse and inclusive political leadership, the nation can advance towards a more representative democracy (Brown & Atske, 2021).

Representation in Congress: The number of Black representatives in the U.S. House of Representatives has increased over the years, reaching a record high in the 117th Congress. In 1965, only five representatives were Black, all belonging to the Democratic Party. Today, there are 57 Black representatives, with two representing the Republican Party. This increase in representation reflects a growing voice for Black Americans in shaping national policies (Brown & Atske, 2021).

Representation in the Senate: While there have been significant achievements in the House of Representatives, Black Americans still face underrepresentation in the Senate. There are three Black senators, the same number as in 2019. Notably, the first Black senator, Hiram R. Revels, served for a year from 1870 to 1871. It was not until 2013 that two Black senators held office simultaneously (Brown & Atske, 2021).

Representation in Governorships: Black Americans have historically faced challenges in securing governorship positions. Currently, no Black governors are in office, with the last Black governor, Deval Patrick, retiring in 2015. Throughout U.S. history, only four Black governors have been elected, serving in Louisiana, Virginia, Massachusetts, and New York.

Representation in Presidential Cabinets: Presidential Cabinets play a crucial role in shaping national policies and priorities. The level of Black representation in Cabinets has varied across administrations. During the Clinton and George W. Bush administrations, as well as Obama's second term, the share of Black Cabinet members was at or above parity with the Black population. However, the Trump administration and Obama's first term saw lower representation, with only one Black

Cabinet secretary in each. With African Americans comprising 24% (6 of 25) of President Biden's full cabinet, this administration showcases a concerted effort to promote diversity, equity, and inclusion at the highest levels.

Conclusion

This chapter has painted a comprehensive picture of the multi-faceted challenges and achievements that define the Black experience in the United States today. From population growth and migration patterns to educational attainment and economic status, the data underscores the resilience and progress within Black communities despite enduring systemic inequities.

The statistics reveal a community that has made significant educational strides, with rising graduation rates and increased enrollment in higher education institutions. Yet, these gains are tempered by persistent disparities in access to quality education and resources. The economic landscape, marked by gradual income growth, still reflects deep-rooted racial wealth gaps that threaten future financial stability. The troubling reality of environmental racism and the disproportionate health impacts of pollution and climate change on Black neighborhoods highlights the urgent need for equitable policy interventions.

Family structure plays a critical role in shaping outcomes for Black children and young adults, influencing everything from educational success to incarceration rates. However, even within similar family structures, Black children face greater challenges compared to their white peers, pointing to broader systemic issues that go beyond family dynamics.

Religious practices and political representation add layers of complexity to the Black American identity. The shifting religious landscape, particularly among younger generations, mirrors broader societal changes, while political advancements showcase both progress and the need for continued efforts toward equitable representation.

As we transition to the next chapter, it is crucial to synthesize these insights into actionable strategies. The following chapter will delve into a SWOT analysis, examining the strengths, weaknesses, opportunities, and threats Black communities face. This analysis will serve as a foundation for developing robust community empowerment strategies to foster resilience, equity, and long-term sustainability. By understanding the intricate dynamics, we can better advocate for policies and initiatives that uplift Black communities and address the systemic barriers that hinder their full potential.

6

Assessing Strengths, Weaknesses, Opportunities, and Threats in Black America

"Not everything that is faced can be changed, but nothing can be changed until it is faced."
James Baldwin

Strengths, Weaknesses, Opportunities, and Threats (SWOT) analysis is a commonly used framework for illuminating organizational strategic pathways. When properly utilized, SWOT is a valuable mechanism for increasing understanding of a community's current state, identifying its challenges and resources, and developing strategies for improvement. As such, organizers frequently utilize this process to determine what is working, what is holding them back, and where resources and energy should be focused to make real progress.

The SWOT analysis process involves four key elements:

- Strengths refer to the internal factors that give a community a competitive advantage or contribute positively to its well-being. These can include community assets, resources, skills, and positive attributes that differentiate the community from others.
- Weaknesses, on the other hand, are the internal factors that hinder a community's progress or contribute to its vulnerabilities. These can include limited resources, inadequate infrastructure, social disparities, or other internal challenges that must be addressed.
- Opportunities are external factors or circumstances that can benefit a community or provide avenues for growth and development. They can arise from economic, social, or environmental changes, policy shifts, technological advancements, or emerging trends. Identifying opportunities allows a community to capitalize on favorable conditions and enhance its potential for positive change.
- Threats are external factors or challenges that pose risks or obstacles to a community's well-being and progress. These include economic downturns, environmental hazards, social unrest, policy changes, and other external pressures. Recognizing and understanding threats is essential for developing strategies to mitigate risks and build community resilience.

The application of SWOT analysis in community contexts has been explored in various studies. For example, D'Onofrio and McIntosh (2018) used SWOT analysis to develop strategies for promoting healthy lifestyles in a remote First Nations community in Canada. They identified community-specific strengths, weaknesses, opportunities, and threats, guiding tailored interventions. Haveman, Goetz, and Renner (2012) applied SWOT analysis to assess community capitals in agricultural contexts, emphasizing the significance of understanding strengths, weaknesses, opportunities, and threats related to community resources. Kuo and Chuang (2018) focused on applying SWOT analysis in community forestry contexts, revealing insights for guiding sustainable forest management practices. Liu, Chen, Wu, and Wang (2020) conducted a study on SWOT analysis in community-based development and low-carbon tourism in Yangshuo, China, identifying strategies for promoting sustainable tourism practices.

These studies demonstrate the versatility and applicability of SWOT analysis in various community contexts, such as health promotion, agriculture, forestry, and tourism. They highlight the value of a comprehensive assessment of strengths, weaknesses, opportunities, and threats to inform decision-making and planning processes. SWOT analysis offers valuable insights and guidance for communities seeking to address challenges, capitalize on resources, and promote sustainable development.

Employing the SWOT analysis process allows community stakeholders to gain valuable insights into the internal and external factors shaping their community. This understanding enables them to make informed decisions, prioritize actions, and collaborate effectively to address community problems and promote positive change.

Analysis of SWOT Results: Understanding Community Dynamics and Challenges

This section examines the findings from the SWOT analysis, breaking down the strengths, weaknesses, opportunities, and threats in detail. It highlights key themes and incorporates participant quotes to provide concrete, real-world examples of community dynamics, illustrating the challenges and pathways to meaningful change.

Informing the SWOT Analysis with Comprehensive Data Sources

The analysis was informed by diverse data sources, including a SWOT questionnaire distributed to residents of 58 majority-Black census tracts, structured interviews, and focus group discussions. These were complemented by national data from the Pew Research Center, adding broader context to African American cultural trends and systemic challenges. This data triangulation enhanced the validity and depth of the findings, ensuring a more nuanced understanding of community dynamics.

The SWOT questionnaire, deployed via Google Forms to 71 Black men and women, provided a broad overview of internal and external factors influencing the community. Structured interviews added depth, capturing personal narratives from individuals with firsthand experience and knowledge of their neighborhoods. These interviews shed light on systemic racism, trust in institutions, community engagement, and visions for change, offering a human dimension to the research.

Focus group discussions further enriched the analysis by fostering dialogue among participants. These collaborative sessions validated and expanded on individual insights, illuminating shared challenges and collective aspirations within the community. These qualitative data sources offered a deeper understanding of Black communities' lived experiences.

Quantitative data from the Pew Research Center (2021) was incorporated to provide additional context, highlighting national trends in Black Americans' experiences and perspectives. This integration offered a macro view to complement the localized insights, enabling a more comprehensive exploration of the issues.

The SWOT Analysis

Strengths

The data yielded from the research highlighted several identified strengths within the Black community. The themes identified included:

Social Cohesion - Unity and Sense of Community: The African American community exemplifies a profound sense of unity and community support, as eloquently expressed by its members. "We all look out for each other," one participant observed, encapsulating the strong kinship that binds community members. This sense of togetherness goes beyond words; it is a palpable force. A shared identity and pride is marked by a genuine willingness to provide mutual support.

This tight-knit community supports one another daily and nurtures entrepreneurship and small businesses. "I see the black community as loving and caring toward people," another participant noted, "We are typically diligent in how we take care of each other's family members and are there to help each other out." This commitment extends to economic empowerment, with community members actively working to uplift each other.

Unity also extends to political activism, where African Americans frequently unite to advocate for social and political change. This spirit of unity is not confined to politics but finds expression in vibrant community events like cookouts and block parties. "The fellowship of coming together for community events like a cookout or block parties are characteristic examples of the African identity's ability to come as a collective group and celebrate one another," said a participant. These events signify the communal spirit, fostering a sense of belonging and shared heritage.

A deep commitment to the community's youth fuels this profound unity. "We all look out for each other," and "We are typically diligent in how we take care of each other's family members and are there to help each other out." This dedication translates into tangible actions, with the community investing time, resources, and mentorship to guide its younger generation toward success. Community organizations are pivotal in offering tailored programs and resources for young individuals. This commitment to community and youth development underscores its unwavering determination to foster positive change within its ranks.

Resilience and Perseverance: The African American community is renowned for its unwavering resilience and remarkable ability to persist in adversity. As one participant eloquently expressed, "We are resilient and extremely innovative. We make a way out of no way and add our flair or flavor to make it shine." Another participant exclaimed, "No matter what obstacles come and go, the black community has a strong sense of community and historic resiliency through the years." This resilience is deeply rooted in the community's history and exemplified by their ability to overcome challenges.

Resilience and perseverance are integral to the African American community's identity. As mentioned, participants consistently highlighted their ability to overcome adversity, innovate, and succeed. "Despite facing systemic barriers, we've always found ways to innovate and thrive, leaning on our creativity and collective strength to progress against the odds." one participant reiterated. Another participant stated, "African Americans have endured so many hardships as individuals and as a community, yet still we continue to bounce back and dominate in everything we do." African American women are collectively viewed as a critical component of the community's resiliency. "An obvious strength of the contemporary (and former) black community is its women," emphasized another participant. The role of African American women in the community's progress and resilience cannot be overstated. Their contributions have been instrumental in shaping the community's identity and strength. This enduring strength is not only historical but continues to shape their response to contemporary challenges.

In times of need, the community rallies together, whether advocating for improved public services or supporting local businesses during challenging times. This collective spirit and commitment to social change demonstrate the community's engagement and activism. As one participant aptly put it, "Our community rallies together in times of need, whether it's advocating for improved public services or supporting local businesses during challenging times." Ultimately, the contemporary African American community draws strength from their collective ability to survive and navigate difficult circumstances. They endure and thrive, turning challenges into opportunities for innovation and growth. As one participant wisely noted, "That kind of community makes a successful person."

Cultural Identity and Influence: The African American community takes great pride in its robust cultural identity, a source of celebration and admiration both within and beyond its boundaries. This identity encompasses various aspects, from their unique language and distinctive mannerisms to their flavorful cuisine and impactful artistic expressions. As one participant aptly put it, "Our sense of culture is strong. It is undeniably beautiful, and its beauty transcends attempts to shame us for it."

This cultural influence extends well beyond the confines of their community, leaving an indelible mark on global popular culture, particularly in the realms of music, art, and fashion. Participants in our study expressed a profound connection to their cultural traditions, highlighting the richness of cultural events and festivals. For them, the community's cultural heritage serves as a wellspring of strength and identity, uniting individuals and instilling a deep sense of belonging in them. As eloquently expressed by one participant, "Our cultural heritage is a source of strength and identity. It unites us and fosters a profound sense of belonging."

Innovation and Adaptability: Innovation and adaptability were identified as key community strengths. Participants in our study boasted of their community's remarkable ability to not only create, as one participant noted, "We do a great job of creating cultural trends that the world adopts," but also to find ingenious solutions when faced with challenges and changing circumstances. This innovation shines through in various aspects of life, from fashion, music, and cuisine to the way they overcome systemic barriers and seize new opportunities. One participant eloquently said, "Our creativity is evident in our hairstyles, fashion, music, and even our food. We have the knack for turning scraps into masterpieces." Such creativity, deeply rooted in the community's identity, is seen as an innate strength, as highlighted by another participant: "Innovation is in our DNA. We find creative solutions to overcome challenges."

This spirit of innovation goes hand in hand with adaptability, enabling the community to forge new paths and overcome obstacles, even in the face of adversity. This is often the work of community-based organizations, as one participant suggested: "We have grassroots organizations that work tirelessly to address social disparities and create opportunities for marginalized groups." Innovation and adaptability represent the African American community's response to adversity.

Weaknesses

In the assessment of weaknesses within the African American community from 2010 to 2020, several critical challenges have come to light:

Economic Stagnation: A foremost concern is the limited economic opportunities available within the community. Many residents express frustration over the lack of job prospects and sustainable income. As one participant candidly put it, "The lack of money is a serious problem." Another participant emphasized that "The African American Community's greatest weakness has always been funding." Participants voiced concerns about the urgent need for more employment opportunities. One participant underscored this issue by stating, "There are few employment opportunities, and many young people have to leave the community to find decent jobs." The barriers to economic mobility and overcoming inequalities were also highlighted. For example, one participant shed light on the difficulty of obtaining credit or business opportunities, noting, "We talk about solving these problems, but if you go start an after-school program, you don't have the credit because you work at McDonald's... if you can distance yourself from your community, then we might allow you to go back and help your community."

Inadequate Infrastructure: Participants also pointed out significant community infrastructure weaknesses. This encompasses concerns about aging public facilities, limited access to reliable transportation, and a shortage of recreational spaces for community members. The absence of well-maintained roads and recreational facilities was seen as negatively impacting the overall quality of life in the community. One participant stressed, "Our community lacks basic infrastructure like well-maintained roads and recreational facilities, which affects our quality of life."

Public Health: Disparities in healthcare access and unequal educational opportunities emerged as widespread concerns. Frustration was expressed regarding the limited availability of healthcare facilities and resources and the unequal distribution of quality education. Participants highlighted the pressing need for improved healthcare services and a more equitable allocation of educational resources. One participant said, "Healthcare services are scarce in our community, and educational resources are not evenly distributed. This puts certain groups at a disadvantage."

Lack of Trust in Local and State Government: A significant weakness identified within the African American community is a pervasive lack of trust in local and state government institutions. This distrust reflects a broader issue of limited linking social capital within African American communities. Participants openly voiced their skepticism, expressing concerns about whether these institutions genuinely prioritize the best interests of their communities. As one participant bluntly stated, "No, I do not trust the local and state government to have the best interest of our communities in mind." Another participant echoed this sentiment, suggesting that the political system offers "little hope for addressing the community's needs." The lack of transparency and accountability in local government further exacerbates this trust deficit.

Pew Research data supports this skepticism, with nearly all Black adults (about 95%) believing that various aspects of the criminal justice system, including policing, the courts, and the prison system, require some level of change to ensure fair treatment. However, despite increased national attention on racial inequality, 65% of Black Americans believe that their lives have not improved, underscoring the community's skepticism towards government actions and reinforcing their call for transparency and tangible improvements.

Lack of Collaboration: Internal divisions and a dearth of collaborative effort represent another formidable challenge to the African American community's progress. One participant succinctly put it, "Our families (and, in turn - individuals) are weakened when community ethics (the standards of conduct) are eroded. We have not been able to reverse our downward slide." Participants consistently emphasized the importance of coming together and collaborating to address their shared challenges. In response to a query about why he and his colleagues did not support local initiatives, one participant lamented, "It's every man for himself." Internal divisions were viewed as a threat, as expressed by another participant: "We are always under the threat of white America further destabilizing our communities because we lack unity and resources." Encouraging collaborative efforts may prove challenging, given that only a minority of people have faith in the collective efficacy of Black people to bring about the change they seek. The Pew Research data indicated that approximately 39% believe that Black ownership of all businesses in Black neighborhoods would be extremely effective, while 31% think the same about establishing a national Black political party. About 27% believe having Black neighborhoods governed entirely by Black elected officials would be highly effective.

Internalized Racism and Cultural Misorientation: The persistence of internalized racism and cultural misorientation issues remains a critical hindrance to progress within the African American community. As one participant poignantly noted, "We are harming ourselves and killing one another, whether it be through unhealthy habits or internal violence." Participants acknowledged the existence of fear and resistance to change within their community. Such fear can obstruct individuals from exploring new possibilities and embracing positive transformation. Additionally, colorism and discrimination contribute to divisions and undermine a sense of unity. Several participants argued that media programming plays a role in driving anti-black behaviors among Black people. One participant aptly observed, "We let the media dictate a lot of our behavior." Addressing internalized racism is paramount for challenging negative self-perceptions and fostering healthier relationships within the community.

Political Apathy and Disillusionment: Many participants expressed a profound sense of apathy and a lack of collective self-efficacy, which may also be rooted in internalized racism and mistrust sown within the community. As one participant noted, "Although we have the capacity to organize, we do not get anything accomplished with our voices. We do not have any leaders who speak for the Black community without their motives." Similarly, another participant stated, "We do not seem to have a sense of accountability in our communities for anything." Disillusionment was evident in the data from the Pew survey, which suggested that only 13% of Black adults believe that equality for Black people in the U.S. is significantly or very likely.

Recognizing these weaknesses allows the African American community to collectively work towards overcoming challenges, fostering unity, and dismantling systemic barriers. By addressing issues of trust, expanding economic opportunities, promoting unity and collaboration, and challenging internalized racism, the community can further empower its members and strive for a more equitable and inclusive future.

Opportunities

The analysis has revealed a multitude of opportunities that hold the potential to fuel growth and development within the African American community:

Economic Empowerment and Entrepreneurship: A significant avenue for growth lies in economic empowerment and entrepreneurship. Participants have underscored the importance of harnessing technology and entrepreneurship to create economic opportunities. Supporting Black-owned businesses is seen as a way to spur economic growth and promote self-determination. Empowering individuals through financial literacy and business education can lead to successful entrepreneurship. Notably, Pew Research data indicates that around six in ten Black adults believe that supporting Black businesses, commonly called "buying Black," is an effective strategy for advancing equality in the U.S. These opportunities enable the community to unlock its economic potential and foster self-sufficiency.

Economic Revitalization: Participants have expressed optimism about economic revitalization within their community. Attracting new industries and businesses has the potential to create local job opportunities, a critical factor in enhancing overall prosperity. The belief is that by drawing in new businesses, the community can generate jobs and improve the well-being of its residents. As one participant aptly noted, "We have untapped potential for economic growth, and by attracting new businesses, we can create jobs and improve our community's prosperity." Moreover, investing in public facilities, enhancing transportation networks, and creating recreational spaces are viewed as avenues to enhance overall livability, attract tourists, and boost the local economy.

Education and Knowledge Sharing: Prioritizing education and knowledge dissemination presents a compelling opportunity for empowerment. Participants have stressed the pivotal role of quality education in equipping youth with the skills and knowledge needed for success. Mentorship programs and access to educational resources can bridge the opportunity gap and empower individuals. By investing in education and knowledge acquisition, the community can play a vital role in addressing disparities and advocating for equal treatment. Expanding educational programs and vocational training has also been recognized as an opportunity to empower community members and address educational inequalities. This expansion aims to provide accessible and relevant education, equipping individuals with the skills required for career success.

Political Engagement and Advocacy: Active political engagement and advocacy have the potential to drive meaningful change. Participants have highlighted the significance of political involvement in addressing the community's needs. Voting and supporting candidates who champion racial justice are regarded as impactful actions. Building coalitions and advocating for policies that promote equal rights and racial justice can shape the future of the African American community. Pew Research data underscores the importance of these opportunities, with the majority of Black adults (85%) considering it crucial to continue making changes to ensure equal rights with White people. These political engagement and advocacy pathways offer avenues for community empowerment and the pursuit of social justice.

Social and Cultural Movements: Social and cultural movements play a pivotal role in raising awareness and fostering discussions about racial inequality. Participants have cited movements like #BlackLivesMatter as exemplary initiatives that have garnered attention and sparked crucial dialogues. Artistic expressions and media representation have the power to challenge stereotypes and reshape narratives, contributing to a more accurate and inclusive portrayal of the African American community. By embracing their history and cultural heritage, the community can reclaim its narrative and empower itself. Pew Research data further supports the impact of these social and cultural movements, with 78% of Black adults believing that the Black Lives Matter movement has heightened awareness of racial inequality. These movements provide opportunities for advocacy, education, and collective action.

Health and Wellness Promotion: Promoting access to quality healthcare and addressing healthcare disparities presents a significant opportunity for the African American community. Participants have emphasized the importance of enhancing overall well-being by investing in mental health resources, destigmatizing mental health issues, and encouraging healthy lifestyle choices. The provision of resources for physical fitness and addressing voting restrictions that disproportionately affect Black individuals are seen as ways to strive for improved health outcomes. These opportunities empower individuals to take control of their health and well-being, addressing systemic issues that have historically disadvantaged the community.

By capitalizing on these opportunities for economic empowerment, education, political engagement, social and cultural movements, and health and wellness, the African American community can make significant strides toward achieving equality, justice, and overall empowerment.

Threats:

The examination of external challenges has illuminated a series of threats that cast shadows over the well-being of the African American community:

Environmental Racism and the Climate Crisis: Concerns about environmental injustices, encompassing natural disasters and pollution, have taken center stage as significant concerns. Participants have voiced apprehensions about the profound implications of climate change and the imperative need for effective disaster preparedness measures to shield residents from harm. The importance of resilience-building efforts has been underscored as a means to safeguard the community. In one participant's words, "Our community stands vulnerable to natural disasters, compelling us to prioritize resilience-building efforts for the protection of our residents."

White Supremacy and Structural Racism: Threats about racism and the enduring influence of white supremacy have been starkly delineated. Participants have shared deeply personal encounters with discrimination, highlighting the pressing urgency to address systemic impediments. The persistent racial inequities that curtail opportunities and engender social divisions within the community have been acknowledged. There's a consensus among participants that dismantling these barriers is an indispensable step toward genuine progress. As one participant cogently asserts, "We grapple with enduring racial inequities that constrict opportunities and breed social divisions. Dismantling these barriers is pivotal for genuine progress." The African American community confronts the grave threat of systemic racism and the persisting ideologies of white supremacy. Participants have emphasized how systemic racism obstructs progress and perpetuates inequality and discrimination.

Additionally, they have underscored the menace that white supremacist ideologies pose to their safety, well-being, and equitable treatment within society. Addressing systemic racism and dismantling the structures of white supremacy are imperative strides toward forging a more equitable future. Pew Research data reveals that approximately half of Black adults regard racism within laws as a more substantial problem than racism perpetuated by individual people. It also shows that 78% of Black adults believe that Black adults receive less fair treatment than White adults in interactions with the police, the courts, and the judicial process.

Capitalism and Class Warfare: Economic disparities and the specter of gentrification have emerged as threats looming over the community. Participants have voiced apprehensions about the surging housing costs and the displacement of long-standing residents, fearing the potential erosion of the diversity and cohesion they cherish. They have emphasized the need for strategic measures to confront economic disparities and forestall the adverse consequences of gentrification. In the words of one participant, "The rapid gentrification unfolding in our community is putting it beyond the reach of many families, imperiling the diversity and cohesion that hold deep value for us." The specters of persistent economic disadvantages, employment discrimination, and financial inequality cast substantial threats upon the African American community. Participants have articulated that these factors obstruct their advancement and curtail opportunities for progress. Addressing the wealth gap and nurturing economic opportunities that uplift the community stand as pivotal imperatives. The dismantling of systemic impediments to economic mobility and financial literacy promotion are identified as empowerment pathways. Pew Research data discloses that 54% of Black adults perceive economic inequality as an extremely or very significant problem for Black people in the U.S.

Cultural Erasure and Mis-education: Participants have expressed a re-sounding insistence that external influences are propagating anti-Black narratives that have detrimental consequences for the community. To counteract these threats, they have stressed the paramount significance of preserving and celebrating their culture, history, and heritage. Promoting accurate representation within education and media has been underscored as an essential strategy to combat stereotypes and elevate the narratives of the community. Confronting the adverse influence of religious teachings and fostering a comprehensive understanding of African American history are recognized as pivotal steps in combating mis-education.

These threats, including systemic racism and white supremacy, economic disadvantage and financial inequality, and cultural erasure and mis-education, spotlight the formidable challenges confronting the African American community in their quest for equality, justice, and empowerment. Addressing these threats necessitates collective action, policy reforms, and an unwavering commitment to dismantling systemic barriers to fashion a more equitable society.

Conclusion

Exploring the current state of Black American communities has revealed the depth of resilience and the magnitude of challenges faced. Despite the significant strides in areas such as education and economic growth, systemic barriers and inequities impede progress. The analysis has highlighted the critical importance of addressing environmental racism, economic disparities, and the ongoing impact of systemic racism on the Black community's well-being.

Having completed the SWOT analysis and gathered extensive data, we now transition to Chapter 7, where we will conduct a structured analysis to synthesize strategic priorities for African American communities. In this next chapter, we will take the insights from the SWOT analysis and systematically identify actionable goals and objectives that will guide our efforts toward community empowerment and sustainable progress.

7

Strategic Priorities for Black Empowerment and Progress

"We are not fighting for integration, nor are we fighting for separation. We are fighting for recognition as human beings." - Malcolm X

In this chapter, I synthesize the SWOT analysis, identifying the key strategic priorities that hold the potential to empower Black communities and drive progress. Recognizing African Americans' various challenges, we focus on strategies with a high probability of success that build upon communities' identified strengths and take advantage of our collective opportunities. These priorities can be used to assist in the development of community action agendas as well as to guide the development of local policy.

Leveraging Strengths to Mitigate Weaknesses

Based on the strengths identified in the community, we can develop strategies to mitigate the weaknesses and address the challenges. Here are some priority strategic approaches:

Community Mobilization: Throughout history, African American institutions have effectively been mobilized to address internal issues. Community mobilization has generally occurred via organized forums, town halls, and task forces that help identify and prioritize critical education, healthcare, and economic development needs. Community-based organizations must continue to create inclusive spaces where community members can actively voice concerns, discuss shared goals, and develop actionable strategies that reflect their collective aspirations. Also, through the promotion of grassroots activism and encouraging community collaboration, we can further enhance these efforts, building social cohesion and empowering residents to take ownership of their community's progress.

Cultural Influence: Furthering the influence of Black culture is a vital priority for strengthening identity and pride within Black communities. Black communities have wielded incredible cultural influence that non-Blacks have utilized to increase their respective influence on mainstream cultures around the world. Therefore, we must improve our ability to weaponize this vital strength. This can be achieved by intentionally organizing cultural events, festivals, and exhibitions celebrating African American heritage, art, and traditions and creating spaces that honor and showcase Black history and culture. Through strategic collaborations with local schools and colleges to incorporate African American history into curricula, we can ensure that the next generation understands and values their cultural roots. Supporting Black community-focused artists, musicians, and writers by providing platforms and amplifying their voices further enriches the community's cultural landscape. Additionally, engaging with media outlets to promote positive and accurate representations of African American experiences fosters a sense of pride and counters harmful stereotypes.

Mitigating Internalized Racism: Internalized racial oppression remains one of the most pervasive challenges for African Americans. In response, Black communities have attempted, with mixed results, to harness their collective power to build cultural movements that reinforce positive self-image, challenge damaging stereotypes, and combat internalized racism. Furthermore, our communities have produced scholars, artists, and activists who have worked tirelessly to address these issues. However, in the absence of the necessary systems change, many of the impacts of internalized racism remain active and debilitating. More widespread action coupled with the intentional organizing of workshops, seminars, and support groups confronting internalized racism to uplift collective self-esteem and foster self-empowerment. Collaboration with mental health professionals to provide culturally sensitive therapy and counseling services ensures that individuals receive support tailored to their unique experiences and challenges. Establishing Emotional Emancipation Circles and mentorship programs connects community members, especially youth, with positive role models who help counteract negative self-perceptions and reinforce a healthy, empowered identity—additionally, promoting media campaigns and educational initiatives that challenge colorism and advocate for recognition of the diversity of the African American experience and reinforces a strong sense of community and solidarity.

Mentorship and Youth Development: Our community has produced a litany of coaches and mentors who have filled critical gaps necessary to develop our youth. We can further this effort by establishing culturally relevant mentorship programs that connect experienced professionals and community leaders with young individuals—with an increased focus on our most vulnerable youth. Offering resources and workshops focused on skill-building, career development, and financial literacy equips young people with essential tools for success and orientates them toward continued community investment. Collaborating with local businesses and organizations to provide internships, apprenticeships, and scholarship programs opens pathways to meaningful career opportunities. Expanding culturally relevant after-school and Saturday School programs offering academic support and mentorship ensures Black youth have access to nurturing environments that foster educational achievement and personal development.

Entrepreneurship and Innovation: An intentional focus on highlighting and supporting diverse approaches to entrepreneurship will prove vital for building economic empowerment and resilience in Black communities. Launching business incubators or accelerators that offer mentorship, funding, and resources to aspiring Black entrepreneurs provides crucial support for new business ventures. Workshops and training sessions on business planning, marketing, and financial management equip entrepreneurs with the knowledge and skills to succeed. Developing culturally relevant curricula on financial literacy and cooperative business models addresses social and economic needs, encouraging sustainable community-based solutions. Organizing networking events that connect Black entrepreneurs with investors and customers—particularly with a focus on cooperatives and community-owned structures—fosters sustained economic empowerment and builds a strong foundation for long-term growth within the community.

Community Education: Our community has dramatically increased learning opportunities for our advanced students. However, it is imperative that we create feedback loops that allow those who benefitted from community support to return to the community and share their skills and information. Collaborating with educational institutions to develop scholarships and mentorship initiatives for African American youth provides pathways to higher education and professional success. Additionally, organizing tutoring programs and workshops to address educational disparities promotes academic achievement, helping students overcome barriers and realize their full potential.

Capitalizing on Opportunities to Mitigate Threats

Using the SWOT Analysis data, we can utilize the identified opportunities to address the various threats facing African American communities. Below are strategies derived from this approach.

Rebuilding Social Trust: Reestablishing social trust in Black communities should start with a focus on repairing the relationship between residents and local institutions. This is best accomplished by advancing ethics reforms that increase transparency and accountability within said institutions. Facilitating community dialogues and forums with local and state government representatives that allow residents to voice concerns, address issues, and participate in decision-making processes that affect their lives will go a long way to repair much of the damage that has been done. In addition, encouraging community members to run for local office and actively participate in governance will empower the community members and ensure that diverse voices are represented. It is also important to continue advocating for policies that increase diversity within government institutions, ensuring that leadership bodies genuinely reflect the community served. Lastly, by supporting initiatives that strengthen police-community relations, such as community policing, implicit bias, anti-racism, and cultural humility training for law enforcement, we can develop cohesive relationships based on mutual respect.

Community-led infrastructure improvements: It is imperative that while we advocate for local municipal bodies to act, we also seek alternative means to improve infrastructure in Black neighborhoods. These improvements are essential for enhancing the quality of life and fostering sustainability in Black communities. Advocating for equitable improvements in infrastructure—such as road repairs, recreational spaces, and sustainable energy solutions like neighborhood solar stations—ensures communities have access to vital resources and safe, well-maintained environments. Expanding community gardens and urban farming projects promotes food security and sustainability and provides green spaces that benefit physical and mental well-being.

Prioritizing Green Jobs and Technology: The growing demand for sustainable economic development presents an opportunity to mitigate threats to our community. It is critical that Black Communities identify sectors with growth potential, such as renewable energy or technology, and push public schools, HBCUs, and Minority Serving Institutions to develop training programs in these areas.

Expanding Collective Knowledge: Expanding communities' collective knowledge base through continuous education may seem cliche, but it is essential for empowering Black communities and preparing future generations for success. Collaborating with schools, colleges, and universities to establish scholarship programs, mentorship initiatives, and educational workshops focused on STEM and high-demand industries opens doors to career opportunities and economic mobility. Advocating for increased funding for Historically Black Colleges and Universities (HBCUs) and promoting diversity across educational institutions strengthens support for Black students and enriches learning environments. Establishing community libraries and resource centers that provide access to books, technology, and educational resources ensures that knowledge and growth are accessible to all, fostering a culture of lifelong learning and empowerment.

Collaborative community planning: Engaging community members in participatory planning can address environmental threats and promote resilience. By establishing community task forces and collaborating with local environmental organizations, Black communities can develop initiatives to reduce pollution, enhance disaster preparedness, and encourage sustainable living practices.

Economic Development Opportunities: Maximizing economic empowerment opportunities is essential for fostering sustainable growth and building wealth within Black communities. By collaborating with local governments and businesses, Black communities can attract industries that align with their needs and values, creating a stable economic base. Advocating for policies that promote equal employment and fair hiring practices will improve employment prospects. Creating worker- and community-owned cooperative businesses can address social and economic goals, fostering shared prosperity and resilience. Expanding job training programs offer community members in-demand skills needed for high-growth industries. Connecting Black-owned businesses with procurement opportunities from larger corporations and government contracts opens up valuable growth channels. Establishing local investment funds and promoting community-led investment initiatives empower Black communities to take advantage of available resources, providing capital to Black-owned businesses and enabling residents to invest directly in their community's economic future.

Political Engagement and Advocacy: To initiate and protect our social and economic advances, we must enhance our political and civic engagement. This can be accomplished by organizing culturally responsive voter registration drives and educational campaigns encouraging active participation in local, state, and national elections. Beyond traditional efforts, developing comprehensive civic engagement plans that include neighborhood-level and community-wide political platforms empowers Black communities to identify and champion their priorities. Building political maturity requires cultivating candidates from within the community who will uphold collective values and advocate for local initiatives. Reserving support and endorsements for candidates prioritizing justice, equity, and progress for Black people strengthens community influence. Finally, fostering inter-community collaborations with other marginalized groups creates powerful coalitions that amplify collective voices and impact advocacy efforts on a broader scale.

Social and Cultural Movements: Black cultural expressions have demonstrated immense social influence and are essential for raising awareness, advocating for justice, and celebrating African American identity. Organizing public demonstrations, marches, and rallies highlights racial inequality and builds momentum for systemic change. Engaging artists, musicians, and activists to create powerful art installations, performances, and media campaigns challenges harmful stereotypes and fosters a deeper understanding of social issues. Supporting community-led initiatives celebrating African American culture—such as film festivals, poetry slams, and historical exhibitions—honors heritage, promotes pride, and reinforces community solidarity.

Health and Wellness: Advocacy is necessary for addressing healthcare disparities and promoting equitable access to health resources in Black communities. Partnering with healthcare providers and nonprofits to establish community health centers ensures affordable and accessible healthcare services for all, addressing vital health needs within underserved areas. Advocating for policies that increase healthcare funding in these communities further strengthens this support, closing gaps in health disparities. Partnering with healthcare providers, community organizations, and government agencies to establish mobile health clinics and affordable clinics provides underserved areas with essential services. Organizing health fairs and workshops focused on preventive care, mental health, and healthy lifestyle choices empowers community members to take charge of their well-being. Collaborating with local fitness centers and wellness programs offers accessible options for physical activity, fostering a holistic approach to health. Advocacy efforts should focus on policies that address systemic healthcare disparities and promote health equity.

Conclusion

By implementing these strategies, Black activists and organizers can leverage strengths, address weaknesses, capitalize on opportunities, and mitigate threats to foster positive change, empower the community, and work towards achieving equality, justice, and overall well-being. In the subsequent chapters, we will use this analysis to inform policy discussions in Chapter 8, exploring how these strategic priorities can shape equitable policies and systemic reforms. In Chapter 9, we will employ these insights to guide grassroots interventions, empowering local communities to take action and drive tangible improvements.

8

Power to the People: Leveraging Democracy to Advance Anti-Racist Policies

"The future belongs to those who prepare for it today." Malcolm X

In this chapter, we will add another layer of synthesis to the SWOT analysis findings by applying the Polarities of Democracy framework. From this framework, we can generate goals and community strategic action items and then recommend government policies intended to mitigate the impact of racism on Black communities. These goals and strategic actions are not intended to be implemented by any specific or single group. Instead, they are general guidelines and aspirations for community-based organizations to utilize in their collaborative efforts. As organizations form and examine their respective missions and agendas, I hope these goals and strategic actions will serve as a framework to advance anti-racist strategic approaches to mitigating racial disparities in American society.

Democracy and Anti-Racist Public Policy

Democracy is best understood as an aspirational form of governance where humans are empowered to participate in collective self-rule. An "effective democracy" moves human societies toward this aspiration by ensuring equitable representation, inclusive participation, social and economic justice, and, at its core, human rights protections for all citizens (Benet, 2013). Democracy has yet to be achieved on a large scale. In the contemporary USA, we seem to be retreating from this ideal, as evidenced by the entrenched systemic racism, worsening economic inequality, and voter suppression tactics, which disproportionately marginalize Black and underserved communities. To advance an effective democracy that mitigates racism, we must recognize how systemic barriers have historically undermined equitable governance. Anti-Racist public policy is critical in dismantling these barriers by addressing racial disparities and fostering an inclusive democratic process that empowers marginalized communities.

The Racism-Community Dysfunction Cycle Theory highlights the complex interplay between systemic racism and community dysfunction, offering a framework to understand and address these challenges. Policies that strengthen democratic structures, such as those promoting equitable representation, transparent governance, and inclusive civic engagement, can disrupt this cycle. My doctoral research (Strouble, 2015) and the Polarities of Democracy (POD) model developed by Benet (2013) emphasize that managing interdependent relationships within democratic governance can provide a robust framework for addressing these systemic issues. Policies designed through this lens must leverage the competing demands of equity and inclusion, individual rights and collective responsibilities, and justice and due process. By navigating these polarities effectively, public policy can enhance our democracy's resilience and its ability to counteract the harmful effects of racism.

Polarities Management and the Polarities of Democracy

The Polarities of Democracy Model

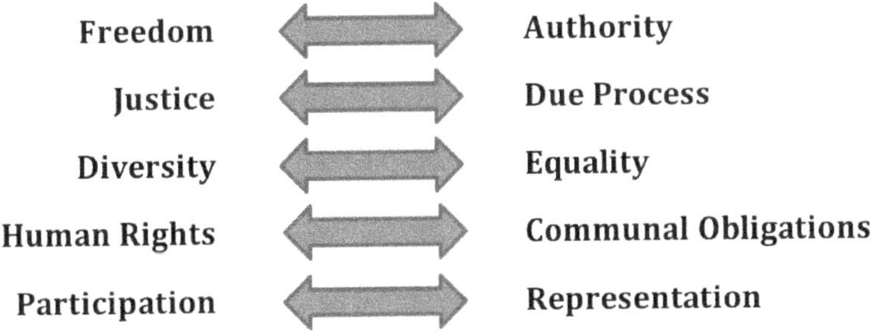

Figure 3: The Polarities of Democracy Theory as an either/or Solution to Oppression, with the Ten values arranged in Their Polarity Relationship
Image reproduced with permission of Polarity Partnerships LLC and the Polarities of Democracy Institute

The Polarities of Democracy model, developed by Benet (2006; 2013), builds upon Johnson's (1996) concept of Polarities Management to improve democratic processes and address complex societal issues. As proposed by Johnson, Polarities Management recognizes the presence of unsolvable problems or dilemmas that require ongoing management rather than simple solutions. It involves identifying interdependent poles and striving to maximize the positive aspects of each pole (Johnson, 1996). Failure to effectively "manage these polarities" can lead to more time experiencing the negative aspects of the pole and less positive experiences (Johnson, 1996). Rather than seeking to eliminate one pole in favor of the other, effective governance involves navigating these polarities to achieve balanced and sustainable outcomes.

Failure to properly manage these polarities can exacerbate societal divisions and perpetuate the downsides of each pole. For instance, an imbalance favoring authority over freedom can lead to authoritarianism, erosion of civil liberties, and social unrest. Conversely, an over-emphasis on freedom at the expense of authority can result in chaos, insecurity, and breakdown of governance structures. In the context of systemic racism, failure to address the tension between diversity and equality, or due process and justice, can perpetuate discriminatory practices, inequitable outcomes, and social injustice.

It is important to note that Benet (2013) vehemently expresses that racism and other forms of oppression are not polarities to manage but instead should be recognized as anti-democratic forces that stifle societies from achieving true democracy (Benet, 2013). Furthermore, racism, like other forms of oppression, is argued by Johnson (1996) to entrap its victims in the downsides of a pole, causing them to pursue the upsides of another pole aggressively. However, the failure to properly manage these polarities will likely result in prolonged experiences of the downsides of each pole. Persistent racial disparities in wealth, health outcomes, educational attainment, and criminal justice highlight the consequences of unbalanced governance, and systemic inequalities are evidence of inadequate management of democratic polarities.

Freedom and Authority

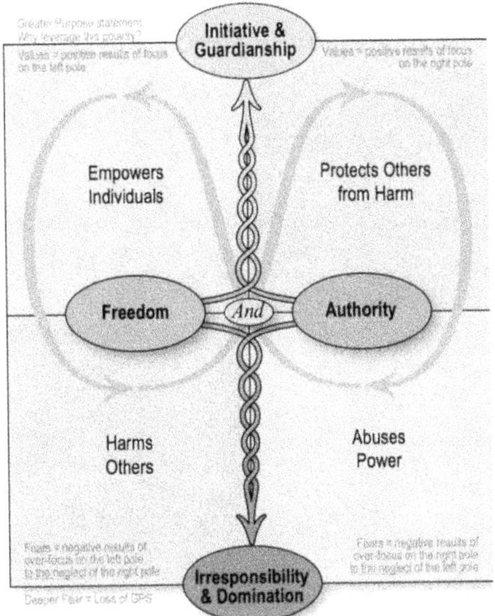

Figure 5: A Polarity Map for Identifying Basic Positive and Negative Aspects of Freedom and Authority

Image reproduced with permission of Polarity Partnerships LLC and the Polarities of Democracy Institute

The polarity between freedom and authority is a cornerstone of democratic governance. Freedom underscores individual liberties, autonomy, and rights, while authority pertains to the legitimate exercise of power and governance by elected officials and institutions. In the context of African American communities, this polarity is evident in debates surrounding civil liberties and law enforcement practices.

In recent years, debates over police conduct and racial profiling have underscored the tension between freedom and authority. Instances of police brutality, such as the killings of George Floyd and Breonna Taylor, sparked nationwide protests calling for greater accountability and reforms in law enforcement practices. However, African Americans remain among the most victimized in the nation by violent crime. Solutions to such a complex problem require effective leveraging of the benefits of authority while safeguarding the freedoms of African American people. Balancing these polarities requires policies that uphold individual freedoms while ensuring that law enforcement operates within the bounds of accountability and respect for civil rights.

Participation and Representation

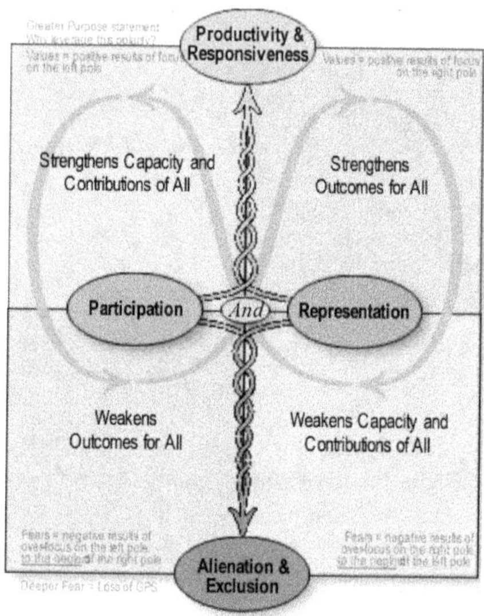

Figure 5: A Polarity Map for Identifying
Basic Positive and Negative Aspects of
Participation and Representation
*Image reproduced with permission of
Polarity Partnerships LLC and the Polarities
of Democracy Institute*

Democratic governance necessitates active participation and inclusive representation to ensure equitable decision-making and policy outcomes. Participation involves civic engagement, activism, and involvement in community initiatives, while representation ensures that diverse voices are heard and integrated into political processes and decision-making bodies.

Historically, African American communities have faced barriers to political participation and representation, including voter suppression tactics and gerrymandering. Efforts to enhance participation and representation include expanding voting rights, promoting census participation, and supporting African American candidates running for political office. However, cronyism or nonauthentic representation are downsides routinely experienced by Black communities when this polarity is not adequately managed. In anti-racist policy formation, advocating for meaningful participation and authentic representation is crucial to effectively addressing systemic inequities and amplifying community concerns.

Due Process and Justice

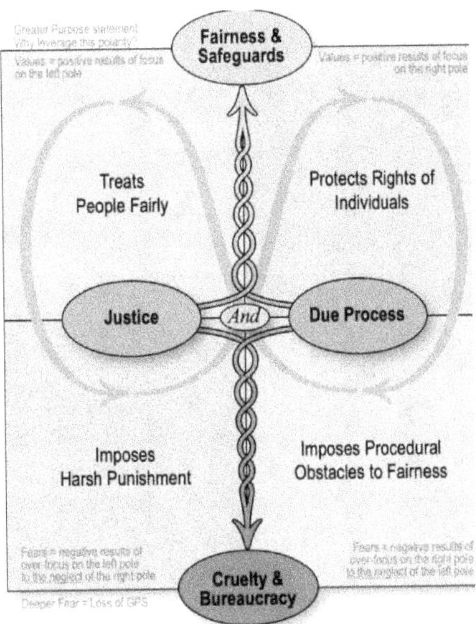

**Figure 6: A Polarity Map for Identifying
Basic Positive and Negative Aspects of
Justice and Due Process**
*Image reproduced with permission of
Polarity Partnerships LLC and the Polarities
of Democracy Institute*

The tension between due process and justice highlights the principles of fairness, accountability, and the rule of law within democratic societies. Due process safeguards individual rights, procedural fairness, and protection against arbitrary actions, while justice demands accountability for injustices, reparative measures, and the promotion of social equity.

In criminal justice reform, African American communities often advocate for reforms that ensure fair treatment under the law and address racial disparities in sentencing and incarceration rates. Initiatives focusing on ending cash bail systems, promoting restorative justice practices, and reforming policing practices aim to uphold due process rights while addressing systemic racism and achieving equitable outcomes in the criminal justice system.

Diversity and Equality

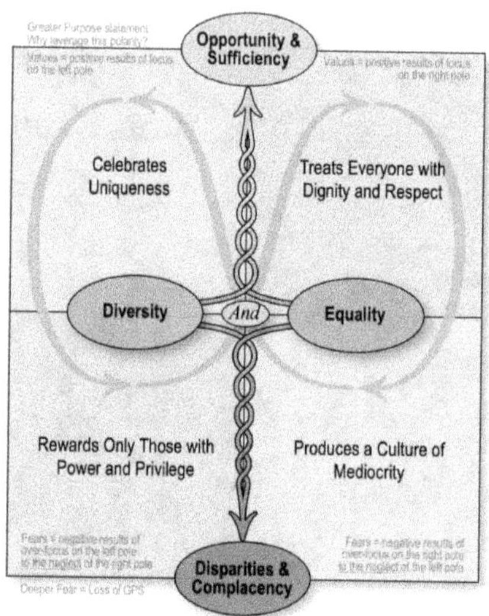

Figure 7: A Polarity Map for Identifying Basic Positive and Negative Aspects of Diversity and Equality
Image reproduced with permission of Polarity Partnerships LLC and the Polarities of Democracy Institute

Diversity celebrates and respects differences in identity, culture, and perspective, fostering inclusivity and representation within democratic societies. Equality emphasizes fairness, non-discrimination, and equitable opportunities for all individuals, regardless of race, ethnicity, or background.

In educational policy, African American communities advocate for policies that promote diversity in school curricula, faculty representation, and equitable access to quality education. Efforts to address racial disparities in educational achievement, funding inequities between schools, and promote culturally responsive teaching strategies aim to reconcile the polarity between diversity and equality. Anti-racist policies in education seek to ensure that all students receive a fair and inclusive learning environment that respects and celebrates their cultural heritage and identities.

Human Rights and Communal Obligations

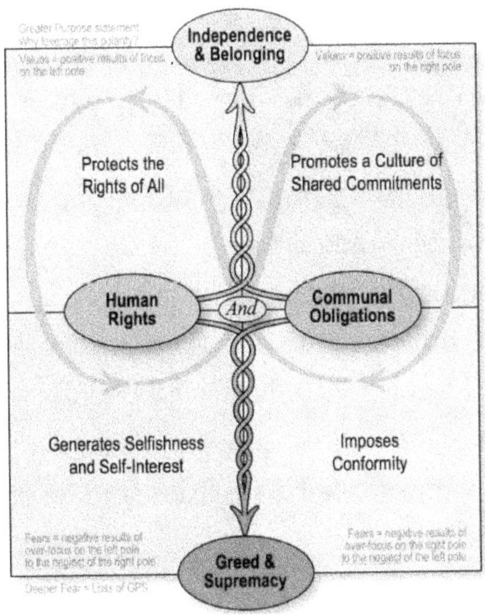

Figure 7: A Polarity Map for Identifying Basic Positive and Negative Aspects of Human Rights and Communal Obligations

Image reproduced with permission of Polarity Partnerships LLC and the Polarities of Democracy Institute

The polarity between human rights and communal obligations explores the balance between individual rights and collective responsibilities within democratic societies. Human rights protect fundamental freedoms, dignity, and equality for all individuals, while communal obligations emphasize shared responsibilities, social cohesion, and the common good.

In healthcare policy, African American communities advocate for policies that ensure access to affordable healthcare, eliminate racial disparities in health outcomes, and promote health equity. Initiatives focusing on expanding Medicaid coverage, addressing environmental factors impacting health, and supporting community health centers aim to uphold human rights while addressing communal obligations to promote health and well-being within marginalized communities.

Forming Anti-Racist Public Policy in Black American Communities

The Polarities of Democracy Model provides a comprehensive analytical framework for advancing democratic governance to address systemic racism. By examining and navigating these polarities, policymakers, advocates, and community leaders can develop informed strategies that promote equity, justice, and inclusivity in Black American communities. Informed by the Polarities of Democracy Model, community leaders, and policymakers can better design, implement, and evaluate policies that allow communities to effectively dismantle systemic barriers, address racial disparities, and foster equitable opportunities for all individuals.

As we navigate the complexities of creating sustainable and resilient communities for Black Americans, it becomes evident that implementing strategic interventions and policy recommendations is essential. These policy recommendations, though broad in scope, serve as starting points that can be adapted to meet the specific needs of local and state contexts. Building on the established baselines outlined in Chapter 5, the SWOT analysis findings from Chapter 6, and relevant examples from historical plans reviewed in Chapter 2, we can now set pragmatic goals and benchmarks and recommended policies to advance progress in African American communities. Again, it is essential to note that these goals, actions, and policies are intended to serve as aspirations for the collective work of African American people and should not be misconstrued as a final destination. Instead, the goals and strategic actions listed in this section should be used to guide planning efforts and policy developments concerning the sustainability and resilience of Black communities.

1. Education and Academic Achievement

Goal: Advance equity and excellence in education by integrating culturally relevant pedagogy, addressing systemic disparities, and equipping African American students with tools for lifelong success.

Targets:

1. Increase African American student's high school graduation rates by 20% in 15 years.
2. Increase African American enrollment in HBCUs by 25% in the next 20 years.
3. Reduce disparity in school readiness for African American students by 30% in 10 years.

Community Strategic Actions:

a. Develop mentorship programs and scholarships tailored for African American students to bridge academic gaps.
b. Establish after-school and summer enrichment programs that focus on STEM and arts, incorporating African American cultural elements.
c. Partner with HBCUs to create dual-enrollment opportunities and college preparatory programs for underserved students.

Policy Recommendations:

i. Increase funding for schools in predominantly African American communities to support improved facilities, qualified teachers, and enhanced educational programs.
ii. Mandate culturally responsive teaching practices and curricula nationwide.
iii. Implement universal preschool programs with targeted outreach to African American families.
iv. Impose financial restrictions on voucher programs and require state governments to offset funds diverted away from public schools.
v. Create incentives and rewards for progress toward reducing racial achievement gaps.

2. Economic Empowerment and Entrepreneurship

Goal: Develop a widespread ecosystem of economic opportunities for African American communities through innovative entrepreneurial pathways, cooperative business structures, and equitable financial resources to close wealth gaps and promote self-determination.

Targets:

1. Increase the number of successful Black-owned cooperative enterprises by 20% in 20 years.
2. Reduce the racial wealth gap between Black and White Americans by 10% within 20 years.

Community Strategic Actions:

a. Create incubators that provide financial support, mentorship, and technical training tailored for cooperative business models, empowering Black entrepreneurs to establish and sustain community-owned enterprises.

b. Develop workshops and certification programs on cooperative principles, governance, and financial planning to equip entrepreneurs with the skills to effectively manage collective businesses.

c. Mobilize community-based investment funds that pool resources to finance cooperative startups and expansions, emphasizing shared ownership and wealth-building opportunities.

Policy Recommendations:

i. Create dedicated federal grant programs and low-interest loan funds for cooperative business models targeting underserved African American communities.

ii. Expand funding for Community Development Financial Institutions to provide capital and technical assistance to African American entrepreneurs, prioritizing cooperative businesses in their lending portfolios.

iii. Offer tax credits to private investors and businesses that provide funding or mentorship to cooperative enterprises in African American communities.

iv. Update regulations to enable credit unions to include cooperative business loans in their portfolios, making them accessible for startups and expansions.

3. Health and Wellness

Goal: Achieve equitable health outcomes by addressing systemic disparities and improving African American communities' access to quality healthcare, preventive resources, and holistic well-being initiatives.

Targets:

1. Decrease the prevalence of chronic diseases, such as diabetes and hypertension, in African American communities by 10% in 20 years.
2. Increase access to quality healthcare services by 15% within 20 years.

Community Strategic Actions:

a. Establish health clinics and mobile health units in underserved areas, providing affordable and culturally responsive care, including chronic disease management, mental health services, and maternal health programs.
b. Develop grassroots educational campaigns and initiatives emphasizing the importance of preventive healthcare practices, including regular check-ups, screenings, and healthy lifestyle choices.
c. Train and deploy community health workers from within African American communities to provide outreach, education, and support tailored to local needs.
d. Support community gardens, urban agriculture, and partnerships with local farmers to improve access to affordable, fresh, and nutritious food options in African American neighborhoods.

Policy Recommendations:

i. Expand access to affordable healthcare and health insurance coverage by implementing state-level health insurance exchanges to reduce financial barriers for low-income African American families.
ii. Invest in community-based health clinics and preventive care programs that target the specific health needs of African

American communities, such as addressing chronic diseases, maternal health disparities, and mental health support.

iii. Allocate federal and state funding for clinics and mobile healthcare units in underserved areas that address chronic diseases, maternal health disparities, and mental health needs.

iv. Introduce policies that increase funding for Supplemental Nutrition Assistance Program (SNAP) benefits, support local food cooperatives, and mandate grocery stores in food deserts.

4. Political Engagement and Advocacy

Goal: Create a politically empowered Black community that drives systemic change through anti-racist policies and establishes a sustainable framework for informed civic engagement and accountability.

Targets:

1. Achieve a 25% increase in African American voter turnout by 2032

2. Establish a process for developing and maintaining national, state, and local - Black political agendas that are recognized and endorsed by 25% of Black Voters in majority Black voting districts by 2032

Community Strategic Actions:

a. Launch targeted voter registration drives, educational workshops, and support services to combat disenfranchisement and enhance civic participation.

b. Establish mechanisms to hold elected officials accountable to their commitments, including public reporting and community forums to assess progress on policy agendas.

c. Provide mentorship, training, and financial support for African Americans seeking office, prioritizing candidates who advocate for locally-driven Black Community Policy Agendas.

d. Create localized and regional platforms that outline vital issues, goals, and policies prioritized by Black voters.

e. Increase grassroots advocacy efforts to challenge voter suppression tactics and advocate for policies that defend and expand voting rights protections.

Policy Recommendations:

i. Enact federal legislation to eliminate voter suppression tactics, including voter ID laws and restrictions on early and absentee voting, while expanding voting access through same-day registration and mail-in ballots.

ii. Mandate independent redistricting commissions to eliminate gerrymandering and ensure fair representation for African American voters.

iii. Advocate for public financing of campaigns to level the playing field for candidates from marginalized communities and reduce reliance on corporate donations that dilute community-driven agendas.

5. Cultural Preservation and Empowerment

Goal: Ensure the equitable representation, preservation, and ownership of African American cultural narratives, with a focus on creating sustainable platforms for Black creators and institutions that amplify Black voices and foster cultural pride.

Targets:

1. Increase Black ownership of media and entertainment companies by 20% in 10 years.

2.   Increase awareness of African American historical achievements and cultural norms by 80% in 10 years.

Community Strategic Actions:

a. Establish a collective fund of 1 Billion Dollars by 2040 to support independent Black filmmakers, artists, and musicians in gaining control over the distribution of their work.
b. Establish 50 new Black cultural preservation centers and museums across the U.S., with an emphasis on underserved regions.
c. Create a network of Black-owned production companies and streaming platforms prioritizing African American stories and employing Black creators.
d. Develop educational initiatives that promote African American history, culture, and achievements within schools and community organizations, encouraging a greater understanding and appreciation of African American heritage.
e. Forge partnerships with cultural organizations, academic institutions, and local community groups to create collaborative programs and events that celebrate African American culture and foster community engagement.
f. Launch media campaigns and advocacy efforts to combat stereotypes, promote inclusive narratives, and showcase the diverse contributions of African Americans to global culture and innovation.

Policy Recommendations

i. Implement federal grants and tax incentives to support Black-owned media companies, production houses, and creative enterprises focused on uplifting African American culture and stories.
ii. Require K-12 and higher education institutions to integrate comprehensive African American history and cultural studies into curricula, emphasizing accuracy and inclusivity.

iii. Establish a federally backed Black Arts Fund to finance artistic and cultural endeavors by Black creators, fostering creative freedom and economic independence.
iv. Support policies that provide Black creators with fair access to digital distribution platforms, ensuring equal visibility and opportunities in global markets.
v. Strengthen legal protections for African American cultural assets, including traditional art forms, historical sites, and intellectual property, to prevent exploitation and cultural erasure.

6. Criminal Justice Reform

Goal: Transform the criminal justice system to ensure fairness, reduce racial disparities, and prioritize community safety and well-being through restorative and equitable practices.

Targets:

1. Achieve a 25% reduction in rates of Black intimate partner violence, murder, drug abuse, arrests, and recidivism within the next 20 years.
2. Reduce negative experiences for African Americans with law enforcement by 20% within 10 years.

Community Strategic Actions:

a. Develop conflict resolution and anger management workshops tailored to the needs of African American communities.
b. Create accessible mental health and trauma support programs for victims of violence, abuse, and systemic injustices.
c. Empower community leaders with mediation and de-escalation skills to resolve disputes, reducing reliance on law enforcement for non-violent conflicts.

d. Introduce school-based initiatives that educate African American youth about their legal rights, responsibilities, and strategies for navigating interactions with law enforcement safely and confidently.

Policy Recommendations:

i. Implement reforms that eliminate cash bail for non-violent offenses, reduce mandatory minimum sentences, and prioritize rehabilitative approaches over punitive measures.
ii. Invest in community policing and law enforcement training programs prioritizing de-escalation, implicit bias training, and community engagement.
iii. Support re-entry programs and initiatives that provide resources and support for formerly incarcerated individuals to reintegrate into their communities and reduce recidivism rates successfully.
iv. Form independent, community-led police oversight boards empowered to monitor law enforcement practices, investigate misconduct, and recommend policy changes.
v. Establish transparent processes for community members to report and address instances of police brutality or misconduct.
vi. Promote restorative justice practices that prioritize rehabilitation and reconciliation over punitive measures, particularly for non-violent offenses and youth.

7. Environmental Justice

Goal: Create equitable environmental conditions for African American communities that ensure fair access to resources and opportunities in the green economy while mitigating the impacts of environmental racism.

Targets:

1. Reduce the exposure of African American communities to environmental hazards by 25% in 20 years.
2. Improve African American access to greenspaces and ecosystem services by 20 in 10 years.
3. Increase African American participation in the Green Economy by 50% in 20 years.

Community Strategic Actions:

a. Support grassroots efforts to advocate for environmental policies that prioritize equity and address historic injustices in African American communities.
b. Implement the closure or retrofitting of industrial plants in Environmental Justice communities, with emphasis on maximizing the reduction of Greenhouse Gas (GHG) and co-pollutants.
c. Support community-led efforts to address environmental justice issues, including grassroots movements, organizing campaigns, and local policy advocacy.
d. Launch programs that promote renewable energy adoption, resource conservation, and waste reduction, creating healthier environments within African American communities.
e. Develop and support educational programs to raise awareness about environmental justice, empowering residents to take active roles in decision-making processes and advocacy.
f. Establish targeted training programs and partnerships with state agencies and educational institutions to ensure African Americans can access high-paying jobs in renewable energy and sustainable infrastructure, such as solar installation and offshore wind development.

Policy Recommendations:

i. Strengthen federal and state environmental laws to prevent industrial pollution and hazardous waste near African American communities, with enforceable penalties for violations.
ii. Mandate equitable distribution of environmental resources, such as parks, tree canopy, green spaces, and clean water in African American neighborhoods through targeted investments and community engagement.
iii. Fund community-led initiatives that focus on environmental justice, including capacity-building programs, environmental health monitoring, and community-driven decision-making processes in environmental policy.
iv. Adopt a federal version of California's Advanced Clean Trucks rule, mandating medium- and heavy-duty vehicle manufacturers to progressively increase sales of zero-emission and near-zero-emission vehicles.

8. Resilience and Climate Adaptation

Goals: Empower African American communities to proactively adapt to climate change and natural disasters by implementing equitable resilience strategies, reducing vulnerabilities, and enhancing recovery capabilities.

Targets:

1. Achieve a 25% reduction in community vulnerability to climate-related events, including floods, heatwaves, and hurricanes, within 20 years.
2. Reduce recovery time for African American communities following natural disasters by 30% within 15 years.
3. Increase African American households' access to renewable energy solutions, such as solar power, by 50% within 20 years.

4. Implement climate education and disaster preparedness programs in 75% of African American neighborhoods by 2035

Community Strategic Actions:

a. Create localized, community-driven adaptation plans that identify vulnerabilities, prioritize actionable strategies, and allocate resources to enhance disaster preparedness, response, and recovery.

b. Increase access to renewable energy within African American communities through projects like solar panel installations, community solar initiatives, and microgrids to lower energy costs and mitigate climate impacts.

c. Promote the adoption of renewable energy sources within African American communities, supporting initiatives that increase access to clean energy, reduce energy costs, and mitigate climate impacts.

d. Launch educational initiatives that equip community members with knowledge and tools to prepare for climate events, adapt to environmental changes, and foster resilience through informed decision-making.

Policy Recommendations:

i. Require federal, state, and local governments to create and implement climate adaptation strategies that prioritize vulnerable African American communities and address their unique risks and resource needs.

ii. Support large-scale projects, such as renewable energy installations, sustainable urban planning, and resilient housing, that strengthen communities against climate change while promoting economic opportunities.

iii. Increase funding and access to community solar projects to reduce energy costs in Black communities and foster energy independence.

iv. Provide grants and technical support to community-based organizations for localized climate adaptation and resilience-building programs, empowering residents to lead in safeguarding their neighborhoods.

9. Affordable Housing and Community Development

Goal: Ensure equitable access to affordable housing, promote sustainable community development, and protect African American neighborhoods from displacement and exploitation, fostering stable and resilient communities.

Targets:

1. Achieve a 20% reduction in unintentional homelessness among African Americans within the next 10 years.
2. Boost African American homeownership rates by 10% within 20 years.
3. Reduce the negative impacts of gentrification on African American neighborhoods by 10% over 20 years.
4. Increase the availability of affordable housing units in African American communities by 25% within 15 years.

Community Strategic Actions

a. Develop programs to educate African Americans at risk of homelessness about available resources, focusing on culturally relevant support services.
b. Establish rental assistance programs and emergency funds to prevent evictions and provide short-term housing solutions.

   c. Partner with financial institutions to provide financial literacy training tailored to African American homebuyers and renters, focusing on wealth-building strategies.

   d. Develop and support community land trusts to empower African American neighborhoods to collectively own and manage land, ensuring stability and resisting displacement.

   e. Provide legal assistance to help African American families address unclear property ownership, combat predatory practices, and navigate property tax disputes.

Policy Recommendations:

   i. Expand mixed-income housing initiatives, inclusionary zoning policies, and programs to preserve affordable housing stock in African American communities.

   ii. Strengthen policies addressing housing discrimination and promote fair lending practices to ensure equitable access to housing resources.

   iii. Allocate funds for community development initiatives, including infrastructure improvements, small business incubators, and the creation of community centers in African American neighborhoods.

   iv. Implement or enhance rent control measures and just-cause eviction protections to safeguard tenants from exploitation.

   v. Fund and provide resources for tenant organizing efforts, enabling renters to advocate for fair housing rights and protections.

   vi. Enforce development guidelines that prioritize affordability, cultural preservation, and active community engagement in planning processes.

   vii. Provide technical assistance and financial support for the creation and expansion of community land trusts to secure long-term land affordability and prevent displacement.

Conclusion

In this chapter, we have completed an in-depth analysis of the SWOT assessment results, further shedding light on the strengths, weaknesses, opportunities, and threats facing Black communities in the United States. Utilizing the insights derived from this assessment, we have laid out a comprehensive framework of goals and strategic actions designed to empower Black communities and foster positive social change. These goals and actions are intended to guide community-based organizations in collaborating and building their unique pathways toward a brighter future.

It is essential to recognize that these goals are not meant to be achieved by any single entity; instead, they provide a foundational blueprint for collective efforts. As organizations and community groups come together, they can use these goals to align their agendas, pool their resources, and work collaboratively towards a shared vision of progress.

The policy recommendations offer a multifaceted approach to addressing the systemic issues affecting Black communities. Education reform, economic empowerment, healthcare access, criminal justice reform, political engagement, housing, environmental justice, and resilience to climate change are all critical areas that demand attention. These federal, state, and local recommendations provide actionable steps for policymakers to dismantle existing barriers and foster equitable opportunities.

Furthermore, exploring the Polarities of Democracy model and the concept of polarities management has illuminated a valuable perspective through which policymakers can address complex societal challenges. By effectively managing these polarities, we can mitigate the negative consequences of unsolvable problems and promote positive outcomes in areas such as justice, participation, representation, and economic opportunity.

As we conclude this chapter, it is important to emphasize that achieving a sustainable future for Black America requires a shared commitment from all segments of society. It demands an unwavering dedication to justice, equality, and eliminating racial disparities. By implementing the recommendations outlined in this chapter and embracing the principles of the Polarities of Democracy, we can move closer to realizing a future where every member of the Black community can thrive, prosper, and contribute to the betterment of our entire planet.

9

Implementing the Vision: Initiatives for Black America's Sustainable Future

"You don't make progress by standing on the sidelines, whimpering and complaining. You make progress by implementing ideas."
Shirley Chisolm

It is unlikely that the polarized political environment in the US will give way in the near future. Should this be the case, Black Communities will have to use multiple strategic maneuvers to advance initiatives that advance us toward our goals of sustainability. Therefore, I propose several community-level intervention initiatives that respond to the SWOT analysis findings in this chapter. Several of these proposals are modified versions of programs I have worked to implement in various communities. These interventions require minimal government or non-local support and can be funded via small grants and/or local fundraising efforts. Furthermore, the resources to implement said programs already exist within African American communities. Ultimately, these interventions are potential first steps in disrupting the cycle of community dysfunction that our prolonged exposure to White Supremacy and Racism has perpetuated.

Intervention 1: Prioritize Community Healing & Emotional Emancipation

The perpetuation of the lie of White superiority and Black inferiority, rooted in centuries of exploitation and dehumanization, continues to shape perceptions and systemic inequalities faced by Black communities worldwide. The impact of racism on the psychological well-being of African descendants underscores the urgent need for community healing and emotional emancipation.

Racial discrimination and daily racial hassles are shared experiences among Black people, leading to adverse psychological outcomes such as distress, depressive symptoms, and diminished well-being (Sellers et al., 2006). These experiences of discrimination can also affect positive psychological attributes, including self-esteem, psychological resilience, and faith in the collective self-efficacy of Black people (Utsey et al., 2000; Sellers et al., 2006).

Cultural factors play a crucial role in shaping identity and buffering the effects of discrimination. Afrocentric cultural values, strong ethnic identity, and positive attitudes toward African Americans have been associated with more positive psychological functioning (Cokley, 2005; Sellers et al., 2006). Creating spaces for Black cultural expression in predominantly Black contexts provides safety and support, counteracting the exoticization and scrutiny often experienced in mainstream society.

Initiatives like the Community Healing Network (CHN) have been established to address the need for emotional emancipation and community healing. CHN focuses on building an infrastructure for complete freedom from the lie of Black inferiority through innovative healing strategies and collaborations. The goal is to empower Black people to move beyond surviving to thrive by healing from the trauma caused by racism (CHN, 2016).

Recognizing the historical context, CHN organized a gathering in Richmond, Virginia, on the 400th anniversary of Africans' first recorded forced arrival in the United States. This event aimed to break the spiritual ties to the past rooted in the lie of Black inferiority and forge a new path driven by the truth of Black humanity (CHN, 2016).

Much of the research that examined the prevalence and impact of racism on African descendants supports the need for emotional emancipation. Initiatives focused on healing and empowering the Black community, including culturally relevant mentoring programs and the promotion of positive racial identity, play a crucial role in combating the effects of discrimination (Belgrave et al., 2011; Sellers et al., 2006; Cokley, 2005).

Launching Emotional Emancipation Circles (EECs)

One effective strategy is the establishment of Emotional Emancipation Circles (EECs). The process begins with engaging the community in discussions about the importance of emotional emancipation and healing. Informational sessions and town hall meetings raise awareness and build support. Community members who exhibit leadership qualities are identified and trained as facilitators, equipped with skills to guide meaningful and healing conversations.

These facilitators then organize the EECs, where participants gather regularly to share experiences, struggles, and emotions related to racism and discrimination. The EECs are designed to be safe, inclusive, and empathetic spaces governed by agreed-upon ground rules that ensure respectful and confidential discussions. Healing practices such as meditation, mindfulness exercises, or art therapy can also be incorporated to promote emotional well-being and resilience. Occasionally, mental health professionals or experts in racial trauma are invited to provide additional insights and guidance for the group.

Annual Community Healing Days Celebration

Complementing the EECs is the organization of an Annual Community Healing Days Celebration. The best way to organize this celebration is to form a diverse event planning committee. The committee leads in selecting themes that reflect healing goals, emotional emancipation, and resilience. The event is then organized to showcase various forms of Black cultural expression, including music, dance, art, and storytelling. Workshops, panel discussions, and strong keynote addresses focused on mental health, emotional well-being, and healing strategies increase the event's effectiveness. It is important to provide attendees with information about local mental health resources, support groups, and counseling services, ensuring access to valuable support networks. The celebration culminates in a collective pledge by attendees to prioritize emotional emancipation, mental health, and community healing in their lives and within the broader community.

Establishing a Mental Health Book Club or Support Group

Another avenue for promoting emotional emancipation is establishing a Mental Health Book Club or Support Group within the community. This group serves as a platform for individuals to engage in meaningful discussions about mental health topics. Books and reading materials are carefully selected to focus on mental health, emotional well-being, and healing from racial trauma, resonating with the experiences of community members.

Scheduling regular meetings allows community members to discuss the readings, share personal insights, and reflect on how the content relates to their lives. The environment is supportive and non-judgmental, encouraging open sharing of thoughts, feelings, and challenges related to mental health. Occasionally, mental health professionals, therapists, or authors of relevant books are invited to join discussions, offering expert perspectives. Members are encouraged to identify actionable steps to prioritize their mental health and emotional well-being, with shared resources and strategies for seeking professional help.

By implementing these initiatives, Black communities can take the necessary steps to actively address the deep-seated wounds caused by racism, promote emotional emancipation, and prioritize mental health and well-being. These efforts collectively challenge the legacy of oppression and contribute to creating a community that recognizes and respects the full humanity of all its members.

Intervention 2: Investing in Culturally Relevant and Anti-Racist Education of Black Youth

Addressing the urgent need for anti-racist and culturally relevant education for Black youth is a community imperative. Considering that these types of programs are barred or avoided in many American public schools, it is imperative that community members take the initiative. A well-designed program can empower students, foster resilience, and chip away at the impacts of systemic racism. These services can be offered after school, on Saturdays, or in winter and summer camps. Here, I outline a specific program model. However, I encourage you to adapt and tailor it to your communities' needs and regional circumstances.

Facilitating Culturally Relevant Learning

Central to this approach is the promotion of culturally relevant learning. This is an excellent opportunity to use culturally appropriate literacy development techniques and enhance students' critical thinking with culturally relevant problem-solving activities. Ultimately, literacy and problem-solving are crucial skills for navigating complex societal challenges.

Creating safe spaces for students to explore their feelings about racism is crucial for building emotional resilience. EECs are helpful in this context as they provide tools for healthy coping mechanisms, allowing youth to process their experiences constructively. Integrating holistic history education through engaging lessons, projects, and book studies ensures that students comprehensively understand their heritage and the societal structures that influence their lives. Additionally, physical health promotion through regular fitness activities builds a positive self-image and reinforces the connection between physical well-being and mental health. Lastly, organizing diverse exposures such as guest speakers and field trips introduces students to various professions and perspectives, expanding their aspirations and understanding of the world.

When possible, the curricula for these programs should be delivered by certified educators and augmented by community leaders and experts. However, considering that the safety of the children is the ultimate priority, strict background checks should be administered to all staff and volunteers. Additionally, when possible, it is very beneficial to employ high school students as mentors and tutors for middle and elementary school students. Ensuring staff is trained in mental health first aid and non-violent communication, coupled with more culturally relevant youth intervention techniques, is also very helpful.

Accessibility

Barriers to participation must be removed for these programs to have a more profound community impact. Transportation access is critical to the program's success. Furthermore, providing nutritious meals ameliorates food insecurity, allows participants to develop healthy eating habits, and contributes to overall wellness. Finally, the program should be offered for free or at minimal cost to students with exceptional vulnerability.

This program model is a prototype for communities seeking to address the need for anti-racist, culturally relevant education for Black youth. The intention is to empower the next generation with the resilience and tools necessary to combat racism and thrive in an equitable society. While these examples are drawn from a structured program, communities are encouraged to adapt and implement actions aligning with their specific regional concerns and unique dynamics. By taking proactive steps toward anti-racist education, we can collaboratively strive for a more inclusive and just future for Black youth, recognizing and nurturing the full potential of every student.

Intervention 3: Cultivating Family Empowerment to Mitigate Cultural Dysfunction

To effectively tackle the pressing issue of cultural dysfunction within our community, it is imperative that we establish programs designed to uplift and empower our families, with a particular emphasis on fathers. This approach is supported by the wealth of research evidencing the significance of fathers in all families, especially Black families. A holistic approach to addressing cultural dysfunction involves the implementation of a Responsible Parenting and Family Development Initiative. This initiative must be meticulously tailored to cater to the diverse needs of participants, encompassing individuals who face various challenges such as low-income circumstances, at-risk situations, high school dropouts, homelessness, receipt of public assistance, non-custodial or custodial parenting roles, refugees, immigrants, active-duty military personnel, veterans, those recently released or soon to be released from foster care, and individuals who have previously interacted with the criminal justice system, including juvenile justice systems.

Program Components

A crucial element of a successful parenting initiative is selecting and implementing evidence-based curricula. This ensures that the program's participants receive guidance grounded in proven methods. Additionally, program facilitators must be adequately trained to deliver content effectively.

The long-term goals of such a program should include enhancing father-child relationships, reducing unemployment or underemployment, strengthening family bonds, developing co-parenting skills, and substantially lowering recidivism rates. It is extremely important to establish a monitoring and evaluation system to track progress toward these goals.

Another critical component of the initiative is forging effective partnerships with local organizations. The program should leverage community resources and expertise by identifying and developing relationships with providers of vital services. Establishing formal alliances and cooperation agreements is a best practice to enhance the program's reach and effectiveness. These collaborations enable a more comprehensive support network for participants, addressing various aspects of their lives and needs.

Ensuring access to a wide range of support services is essential for addressing participants' multifaceted challenges. The program creates a network of services encompassing educational support, housing assistance, employment opportunities, and more. Clear pathways are necessary for participants to access these services. This integrated approach facilitates holistic support, empowering participants to overcome obstacles and achieve stability.

It is vital to recognize and remove barriers to program participation and success. Routine evaluations to identify potential obstacles such as transportation issues, childcare needs, or scheduling conflicts are helpful. Strategies should then be developed to eliminate or mitigate these barriers, ensuring they do not hinder participants from fully engaging with the program.

Training and equipping program staff with the necessary skills is fundamental to the initiative's success. Skilled and empathetic staff can better build participant trust, fostering a supportive environment conducive to positive change. Staff must receive comprehensive training in cultural competency, case management, and effective facilitation. Providing ongoing professional development opportunities will ensure the team remains well-prepared to deliver high-quality services.

The development of Parenting and Family Development Initiatives, guided by these specific program objectives, represents a robust and inclusive approach to addressing cultural dysfunction by empowering fathers and strengthening family units. By prioritizing responsible parenting, economic stability, healthy marriages, and re-entry support, we aim to foster a more resilient community where families thrive, thereby driving positive cultural transformation.

Intervention 4: Using Cultural Policy to Build Black Social Capital

Restoring Social Capital, or Ubuntu, requires a conscious, collective, and informed effort by Black leadership across generations. This effort starts with the study of history and debunking the myth of Black inferiority (Jackson-Lowman, 2016).

Cultural standards grounded in the values and principles of Ubuntu, accompanied by cultural policies that articulate expected behaviors within the community, are proposed as a liberatory catalyst for addressing the effects of forced displacements and ending cultural oppression. This involves using various forms of media, social, political, and religious organizations, historically Black colleges and universities, and Black-owned businesses to promote Ubuntu values and hold each other accountable for their implementation (Jackson-Lowman, 2016).

Developing cultural policies is crucial for organizing the African American community's knowledge, skills, resources, and energies around a culturally relevant socialization process for Black children. This seven-step process includes:

1. Identify specific cultural policies that align with Ubuntu's values and principles. Policies may promote educational equity, community engagement, or economic empowerment.
2. Create a strategy to effectively communicate these cultural policies within the community. Disseminate information through various communication channels, such as community meetings, social media, or newsletters.
3. Determine the most effective methods for promoting and implementing these cultural policies. This could involve partnerships with local organizations, educational programs, or awareness campaigns.
4. Clearly outline the expected behaviors and actions that align with the cultural policies. For example, if the policy focuses on education, the expected behavior might include parents actively participating in their children's schooling.
5. Establish mechanisms for monitoring and measuring the progress of cultural policy implementation. This could involve regular assessments, surveys, or feedback from community members.
6. Incorporate cultural rituals and practices that reinforce the values embedded in these policies. These rituals can be powerful reminders of the community's commitment to these principles.
7. Periodically assess the impact and effectiveness of these cultural policies. Are they achieving the intended outcomes? Are there areas that require adjustments or improvements?

While there is little research on best practices for enforcing cultural policy, I have identified a few community-scale enforcement approaches. These enforcement mechanisms can include:

- Establish councils or committees responsible for overseeing the implementation of cultural policies and addressing any violations or concerns within the community.
- Promote a culture of peer accountability, where community members hold each other responsible for adhering to the cultural policies.
- Conduct educational programs and workshops to ensure that community members understand the significance of cultural policies and the positive impact they can have.
- Set up confidential reporting mechanisms for community members to report policy violations or concerns without fear of reprisal.
- Recognize and reward individuals or groups within the community that actively contribute to promoting and implementing cultural policies.

Cultural policies serve as a collective reminder and responsibility to socialize Black children and foster a sense of connectedness and commitment within the community (Jackson-Lowman & Haile, 2016). By embracing cultural policies that reflect the excellence and potential of Black American youth, the community challenges the "inferiorization" process and cultural misorientation, fostering self-determination and unity. Cultural policy becomes a means to restore the village concept and raise healthy, secure, and well-functioning Black American youth (Jackson-Lowman & Haile, 2016).

Intervention 5: Harnessing Community-Based Participatory Methods to Boost Black Social Capital & Resilience

Researchers and planners can play a crucial role in advancing solutions for communities grappling with multifaceted challenges. Community-based participatory methods have proven transformative in such circumstances. By actively involving community members in planning and research efforts, researchers and communities can co-develop tailored strategies that acknowledge a community's specific needs and vulnerabilities while leveraging their inherent strengths. This approach is amazingly efficient in revitalizing social capital within Black communities.

Community-Based Participatory Research (CBPR) is a potent instrument for addressing urban health disparities and championing equitable outcomes in Black American communities. This approach actively involves community members as research partners, acknowledging their expertise and valuing their life experiences. CBPR empowers the identification of community-specific avenues for change and the formulation of targeted interventions to combat the challenges facing Black American communities. By conducting research collaboratively, with robust community partnerships, researchers can ensure that the findings are meaningful, relevant, and actionable.

Research processes need to be flexible to realize the genuine application of CBPR. This entails adapting methodologies to align with the cultural context, employing culturally sensitive data collection techniques, and actively engaging community members in data interpretation and dissemination. By aligning research endeavors with community priorities, CBPR emerges as a catalyst for change, offering vital support for the revival and resilience of Black American communities.

In addition to CBPR, Community-Based Disaster Resilience Planning (CBDRP) is gaining prominence as an essential paradigm for disaster planning. (Eisenman, Adams, & Rivard 2016). This planning methodology complements traditional efforts to fortify physical infrastructure and upgrade disaster-related technologies (Flanagan et al. 2011). It operates through multifaceted, community-sensitive approaches that are adaptable to various hazards. Programs should be tailored to address Black communities' most pressing threats.

Such programs carry significant potential for diminishing risk and enhancing resilience by diversifying and strengthening social capital and communication networks. They also encourage group-based preparedness planning and identifying other resilience-enhancing strategies, accomplished through the collaboration of residents, policymakers, and local institutions. This comprehensive engagement will heighten preparedness, enrich social capital, diversify communication networks, and, most importantly, enhance the resources available for mitigating vulnerability within Black communities.

Potential Program Model

In a community participatory model, sustained and iterative engagement is paramount, with equitable distribution of participation levels (Balazs & Morello-Frosch, 2013). Additionally, it is crucial to incentivize participation, acknowledging the time and effort community members contribute at various project stages.

1. **Community Entry Protocols:** Engagement begins with community entry, where the initial research team immerses itself in the selected communities. The aim is to understand community needs and issues while identifying gatekeepers, often through preexisting nonprofit organizations, community-based groups, and local officials. To safeguard community interests, the Action Team (AT) enters into a memorandum of agreement with AT members. The subsequent step involves soliciting participation from residents through an outreach campaign that informs them about the program, its objectives, and participation opportunities. An integral aspect of this phase is integrating community members into the research and planning process.

2. **Orientating Community Members:** The program commences with an Orientation Meeting designed to introduce residents to the project and the Action Team (AT). Simultaneously, the AT diligently prepares training materials and conducts comprehensive training sessions to equip data collectors with the requisite skills for qualitative data collection.

3. **Pre-intervention Data Collection:** Collecting pre-intervention data is the foundation for evaluating the project's effectiveness. Various data collection instruments are employed to achieve this, with AT members taking the lead. A culturally responsive assessment tool should be utilized to gather data on diverse resilience indicators through community meetings. The assessment encompasses household and community-scale preparedness surveys, asset mapping, and an assessment of the use and accessibility of information channels. Additionally, participatory mapping is employed to identify community assets and vulnerabilities. It is also beneficial to assess cognitive social capital elements linked to disaster response, such as social trust, collective efficacy, and civic engagement. Semi-structured interviews help explore resilience perceptions and examine the selected neighborhoods' social infrastructure. Potential disaster response scenarios are employed to elicit responses from community members.

4. **Community Intervention:** A comprehensive series of activities should be implemented to fortify social capital within the community and bolster resilience. The primary goal is to design disaster resilience plans tailored to each neighborhood's specific conditions and needs. These plans include maps that facilitate the communication of risks and assets. It is crucial that these plans address opportunities to strengthen bonding, bridging, or linking social capital in ways that enhance resilience against pertinent community challenges. The final planning process is developed collaboratively with the AT and relevant local officials.

5. **Community Exit:** Participants are reconvened to discuss their experiences, and draft reports are shared to gather feedback before formal publications. An essential aspect of the exit phase involves collaboratively determining the next steps in the resilience plan implementation process, potentially leading to the formation of organizational structures.

6. **Closing the Program:** The resilience planning process commences with a review of findings from the pre-intervention assessments. The AT then develops a neighborhood resilience plan template, including methods for prioritizing improvement strategies and essential implementation steps. An effective plan also identifies information channels and critical social links. Subsequently, the draft neighborhood resilience plans undergo a thorough evaluation by the AT and community members. In the final stages, community members present their plans to other stakeholders, including emergency management and public officials. These preliminary plans should be adjusted as necessary.

Revitalizing Black American communities necessitates a proactive approach that centers on rebuilding social capital, fostering community engagement, and implementing community-based participatory research. Investing in these communities' strengths and potential and addressing systemic barriers can pave the way for resilience, empowerment, and sustainable development. Through targeted strategies, inclusive planning processes, and collaborative research, we can support the restoration of Black American communities, advocate for social justice, and contribute to a more equitable society.

Intervention 6: Intentional Black Sustainability and Resilience:

Advancing sustainability in Black American communities requires innovative strategies focusing on localized economic development, workforce training, and infrastructure improvement. By adopting approaches rooted in community empowerment, environmental justice, and collaboration, Black communities can address the impacts of environmental racism and build resilience.

Environmental issues such as poor air quality, limited access to fresh food, inadequate clean energy, and insufficient green spaces are exacerbated by a lack of economic opportunities and underdeveloped infrastructure. Tackling these challenges necessitates the cultivation of well-trained community advocates who are intimately familiar with local assets and committed to defending and enhancing their neighborhoods.

Central to this initiative is forming organized community response teams. These groups can lead environmental stewardship, data collection, and community engagement efforts. The process starts by identifying and recruiting community members, particularly youth passionate about environmental justice and sustainability. Partnerships with local schools, community centers, and organizations will assist with reaching individuals deeply connected to the neighborhood.

Next, it is best to provide comprehensive training from local experts in areas such as air and water quality monitoring, soil analysis, recycling initiatives, urban agriculture, energy conservation, and leadership development. Consistent with the principles of CBPR, participants should be compensated when possible. Once trained, these members should actively engage with residents to address immediate environmental concerns, collect valuable data, and advocate for sustainable practices. They become catalysts for positive change, empowering their neighborhoods from within.

Involving the community in data collection and reporting is fundamental to creating impactful solutions. Collaborations with local academic institutions, including Historically Black Colleges and Universities (HBCUs), enhance the credibility and effectiveness of the findings. Geographic Information Systems (GIS) should be used to create dynamic maps highlighting tangible assets like local businesses and public facilities and intangible treasures such as cultural heritage and traditions. These visual tools help identify strengths and areas for improvement. Presenting the findings to local authorities and relevant government agencies ensures that community voices are amplified and proposed solutions align with local needs and priorities.

Developing a comprehensive Community Sustainability Plan guides long-term environmental justice and resilience efforts. This process involves initiating a strategic planning phase that actively includes community members. Open forums, workshops, and brainstorming sessions are held to gather input on environmental goals and practical strategies. Creating an inclusive atmosphere where diverse voices contribute to the plan's development is essential, and residents are encouraged to share their aspirations and concerns.

Engaging local environmentalists, urban planners, and sustainability experts brings valuable insights into sustainable practices and technologies suited to the community. Again, collaborations with nearby educational institutions, especially HBCUs, allow local residents to break through the ivory tower and access academic expertise. This approach also involves college students in local sustainability initiatives, establishing the "town to gown" connections. Partnerships with community-based organizations that understand the unique challenges and opportunities within Black communities ensure that programs are culturally relevant and effectively address local issues.

Building close relationships with local government agencies is crucial. Elected officials, city planners, and environmental departments should actively participate in the sustainability planning process, aligning policies and regulations with community goals. Their support is instrumental in ensuring the plan's successful implementation.

Once the sustainability plan is finalized, celebrating this milestone with a community-wide event fosters a sense of ownership and pride among residents. Events like Earth Day or Community Healing Days are excellent opportunities for such celebrations. The aim is to unite the community to recognize their achievements and showcase the plan's key elements and objectives through visual presentations and interactive displays. Recognizing the contributions of community members,

Green Teams, and Climate Corps members who played vital roles in the planning process highlights their dedication and commitment to a sustainable future.

Key elements of the sustainability plan effectively address critical areas. Green Workforce Development focuses on establishing Green Corps programs to hire and train Black youth in invasive species removal, tree planting and maintenance, and climate-mitigating landscaping improvements. Providing pathways for participants to earn certifications enhances employability in green industries. Fee-for-service activities generate revenue, sustain the program, and provide economic opportunities.

Residential and Community Gardens & Urban Farms involve incentivizing residents to establish and maintain gardens through grants, resources, or recognition programs. Facilitating bartering and needs-based exchanges strengthens local food networks and builds community cohesion. Collaborations with schools, restaurants, and grocers develop Community-Supported Agriculture (CSA) programs, providing fresh produce and supporting local economies. Working with urban farmers supplies locally grown produce to schools and markets, fostering healthier eating habits and supporting local economies.

Implementing Collective Carbon Sequestration Strategies educates residents about the importance of carbon sequestration and its impact on environmental health and community well-being. Incentivizing the creation of microforests and food forests offers environmental benefits and food resources. Promoting initiatives that maintain green spaces, prevent urban blight, and improve air quality are integral to this component. Culturally relevant marketing resonates with the community, explaining the significance of these initiatives and emphasizing benefits like reduced urban heat, improved air quality, and enhanced neighborhood aesthetics.

Advocating for Equitable Clean Energy Transitions is also essential. Promoting access to renewable energy sources such as solar and wind power supports initiatives that make sustainable energy practices affordable. Encouraging energy-efficient practices in homes and businesses by providing resources, education, and incentives helps reduce consumption and lower utility costs.

Establishing Air and Water Quality Monitoring involves community-led efforts to inform residents about environmental conditions. Providing tools and education empowers community members to interpret data and advocate for environmental health. This transparency fosters trust and encourages active participation in environmental stewardship.

Amplifying the program's impact through a dynamic social media campaign educates and engages the broader community about environmental justice. Sharing success stories, interviews with experts, and the progress of Green Teams and Climate Corps members through social media channels, partner websites, and community forums raises awareness. Partnerships with local media outlets, community influencers, and organizations expand the campaign's reach and engage a broader audience.

Establishing an evaluation framework ensures the program's ongoing success and relevance. Regular evaluations using data analysis, surveys, and community feedback measure progress toward goals. Being prepared to adjust strategies in response to emerging needs, challenges, and opportunities is vital. Sharing evaluation results with the community maintains transparency, fosters trust, and encourages continued participation.

By following this comprehensive framework and adapting it to region-specific circumstances, communities can develop tailored programs that enhance Black resilience and sustainability. The key to success is fostering community engagement, leveraging local expertise, and promoting collaboration to create positive, lasting change that advances environmental justice and equity.

Starting with one or two of the community's most relevant and achievable initiatives builds momentum. Early successes generate enthusiasm and attract more participants and partners. Seeking funding and support through grants, sponsorships, and partnerships secures the necessary resources for program expansion. Open communication within the community and with external stakeholders sustains engagement and support.

Embracing these strategies enables underserved Black American communities to address immediate environmental and economic challenges while laying the groundwork for long-term growth and empowerment. Proactive efforts contribute to a legacy of resilience and prosperity for future generations, fostering a healthier, more prosperous future for all community members.

Intervention 7: Practicing Collective Civic Engagement

Empowering and engaging members of the Black community while building political power and self-reliance requires innovative approaches that broaden participation beyond traditional methods. This comprehensive initiative is designed to strengthen political engagement and foster self-determination within the community.

At the heart of this strategy is the diversification of engagement networks. It begins with identifying cherished community spaces such as barbershops, community centers, churches, and religious institutions. These venues serve as foundational hubs for engagement, and tailoring approaches based on community feedback can enhance their effectiveness. Beyond these traditional spaces, exploring unconventional venues like clubs, lounges, sporting events, social gatherings, and storefronts can open new avenues for connection. Collaborating with community experts helps pinpoint the most promising locations for unique engagement opportunities.

Embracing the digital age is also crucial. Hosting virtual town halls on social media platforms increases accessibility and participation, allowing community members to engage from the comfort of their homes and strengthening connections between Black community members on local college campuses and those residing in neighborhoods fosters cooperation and communication, bridging generational and experiential gaps. Active grassroots organizing within neighborhoods is pivotal for building connections and amplifying voices, ensuring that engagement is rooted in the lived experiences of community members.

Utilizing empowerment messaging is another crucial component of the initiative. Crafting messages that emphasize the inherent power and capabilities within the Black community fosters a sense of strength and self-determination. The community can showcase constructive contributions and nurture pride and stewardship by shifting narratives to highlight positive stories and successes. Ensuring that messaging is culturally relevant and resonates with the experiences and values of the Black community makes it more relatable and meaningful.

Facilitating community-participatory decision-making actively involves community members in shaping the direction and initiatives of projects. This includes prioritizing platform development, town hall meetings, candidate forums, and other engagement opportunities that align with specific needs and concerns. Inclusive decision-making empowers individuals, giving them a stake in the outcomes and fostering greater commitment to collective goals.

Incentivizing peer-to-peer engagement is a powerful strategy to motivate action. Developing innovative programs that empower and incentivize aspiring community leaders encourages them to take influential roles in driving transformative change. Offering comprehensive civic engagement training, possibly with stipends to recognize their commitment, equips participants with the knowledge and skills needed for effective advocacy. Performance-based incentives, such as cash bonuses tied to key civic engagement actions like voter registration, campaign contributions, volunteering, attending civic education workshops, giving public comments, and engaging with candidates, further motivate sustained participation.

Suggested Program Objectives

1: Enhanced Civic Education

The first objective is to develop and implement an educational curriculum focused on local politics and community political strategy.

The program aims to increase political knowledge within the Black community by conducting educational workshops and town halls and empowering individuals to engage more effectively in the political process.

2: Organized for Empowerment

Recruiting and training a group of Community Empowerment Organizers (CEOs) is essential for engaging community members in targeted civic actions. Establishing a community participatory candidate review process allows for assessing local policies and candidates, ensuring they align with the community's interests. Developing and distributing empowerment-oriented messaging encourages community members to take targeted civic actions, fostering a collective movement toward empowerment.

3: Enhanced Black Engagement with Local Politics

Developing a Black Community Policy Platform with the support of community members provides a unified vision and set of priorities. Organizing candidate forums engages the community directly with political candidates, facilitating dialogue and accountability. Facilitating coordinated participation in supporting candidates' campaigns, potentially utilizing programs like the City of Tallahassee's Campaign Contribution Reimbursement Program, increases the community's political influence. Recruiting volunteers for various campaign activities further amplifies engagement and impact.

4: Evaluate and Document Findings

Conducting routine internal evaluations assesses program effectiveness and identifies areas for improvement. External evaluations provide objective assessments of the initiative's impact. Identifying best practices for scalability and replication in similarly situated areas ensures that successful strategies can be extended beyond the initial community. Creating a comprehensive program report documents findings, insights, and lessons learned, providing valuable resources for future initiatives. Planning for future iterations of the initiative continues the momentum, further empowering and engaging the Black community.

This adaptive model empowers the Black community by enhancing political knowledge, encouraging sustained participation, and fostering involvement in decision-making and policy advocacy. Diversifying engagement methods, adopting positive and culturally relevant messaging, fostering participatory decision-making, and incentivizing peer-driven action can create a powerful movement.

This blueprint is particularly suitable for moderately organized Black communities seeking to enhance their collective civic engagement and political influence. Communities are encouraged to adapt these components to their specific needs and set target engagement ranges based on their goals. By taking proactive steps to empower community members and build political power, the initiative contributes to increased self-reliance and a stronger voice in the political arena, ultimately driving transformative change.

Intervention 8: Resisting Gentrification and Preventing Displacement

In an era defined by urban renewal, neighborhood transformation, and rapid demographic shifts, the threat of gentrification looms large over many historic Black communities. Driven by capitalist interests and often propelled by systemic inequalities, gentrification poses a significant challenge to these neighborhoods' essence and existence. Black communities have been pillars of resilience, culture, and history for generations. They have endured hardships, discrimination, and systemic racism, emerging more potent and more vibrant with each trial. Yet, if unchecked, the tide of gentrification threatens to erode their foundations, dispersing residents and erasing the rich tapestry of their cultural heritage.

To combat the encroachment of gentrification and prevent the serial forced displacement of Black residents, intentional programs must be established. These initiatives must go beyond mere reaction and resistance; they must be proactive, empowering, and rooted in community collective ownership, economic empowerment, and cultural preservation. Recognizing that gentrification is not an inevitable force of nature but a consequence of complex societal structures, such programs should be designed to address the systemic racism, discriminatory policies, and economic disparities that have made Black communities vulnerable. At this critical juncture, we must act with purpose and conviction to ensure that neighborhoods serving as havens of Black culture, identity, and solidarity remain intact.

One such initiative is the "Community Legacy Guardians," designed to empower Black communities by providing them with tools and resources to resist gentrification, maintain ownership of their neighborhoods, and preserve their cultural heritage. This program focuses on community collective ownership, community land trusts, and cultural preservation efforts.

Central to the initiative is establishing Community Land Trusts (CLTs) in targeted neighborhoods. These trusts hold community-owned land in perpetuity for the benefit of current and future residents. Establishing a CLT board composed of residents, experts, and advocates will help the community retain oversight and control over land trust operations. This ensures that land remains in the hands of those who live there, preventing outside interests from displacing residents.

Collective economic empowerment is another cornerstone of the program. Facilitating the establishment of community-owned businesses and cooperatives provides jobs and opportunities for residents, developing economic stability. Promoting financial literacy and entrepreneurship programs helps residents build wealth collectively, reducing the economic vulnerabilities that gentrification often exploits. When appropriate, establish community development corporations that allow for the pooling of resources to advance home repairs and weatherization efforts and provide emergency relief to members at risk of losing their property.

Equally vital are efforts in cultural preservation. Creating cultural preservation committees allows communities to document, celebrate, and protect their rich heritage. Collaborations with local artists, historians, and cultural experts lead to the development of cultural programs and events that reinforce community identity and pride.

Addressing housing concerns, the initiative emphasizes affordable housing initiatives to ensure residents are not priced out of their neighborhoods. Developing affordable housing projects within the community maintains accessibility for all income levels. Advocating for and negotiating with developers to set aside portions of new developments as affordable housing units helps integrate new growth without displacing existing residents.

Legal and policy support offers residents the necessary tools to combat eviction or displacement. This is extremely important in the context of heirs' property cases. Legal advocacy services protect tenants' rights while pushing for policy changes at local and state levels to prevent unjust property tax increases and other practices that facilitate gentrification.

Community engagement and education form the backbone of the initiative's success. Organizing regular community meetings and workshops educates residents about the threats of gentrification and the tools available to resist it. Encouraging active participation in decision-making processes related to land use, zoning, and development empowers the community to have a say in their neighborhood's future.

The initiative includes youth and education programs to ensure sustainability. Establishing educational programs and mentorship opportunities for young residents focuses on cultural preservation and community history. Encouraging youth leadership and involvement fosters a new generation committed to protecting and enhancing their community.

Lastly, forging collaborations and partnerships extends the initiative's reach and effectiveness. The community can leverage additional resources and support by partnering with local non-profit organizations, academic institutions, and government agencies. Collaborating with neighboring communities facing similar challenges allows for sharing best practices and creating a united front against gentrification.

Measuring the success of these initiatives involves several factors. The number of properties acquired by the Community Land Trust indicates the community's level of control over its land. An increase in affordable housing units ensures residents can remain in their neighborhoods. Growth in community-owned businesses and cooperatives reflects economic empowerment. Successful preservation of cultural heritage through documented events and programs maintains the community's identity. A decrease in eviction rates and displacement signifies effective resistance against gentrification. Heightened community engagement and active participation in decision-making demonstrate a robust and unified community ready to shape its destiny.

The "Community Legacy Guardians" initiative aims to empower Black communities to take control of their future, resist gentrification, and ensure that their neighborhoods remain vibrant, culturally rich, and economically viable for future generations. It requires collaborative efforts, community engagement, and a commitment to collective ownership and preservation. Through these concerted actions, communities can stand resilient against the forces that threaten their existence, preserving their heritage and securing a prosperous future.

Intervention 9: Assessing the Need for Strategic Relocation

In certain circumstances, Black Americans may face the difficult decision of whether to abandon specific communities and cut their losses. While community revitalization and restoration are essential goals, there are instances where the systemic challenges and barriers may be insurmountable, rendering strategic relocation a viable option. When members of your community are so inundated by racism and White supremacy that you cannot begin the work to restore your community to basic functionality, it may mean it is time to choose strategic relocation. This section examines the factors that may necessitate such decisions and provides a framework for assessing the need for community transitions.

Systemic Inequities and Disinvestment: Many Black communities have long been subjected to systemic inequities, disinvestment, and neglect. This can manifest in various forms, such as inadequate infrastructure, limited economic opportunities, inadequate access to quality education and healthcare, and disproportionate exposure to environmental hazards. When these challenges persist despite efforts for change, it may be necessary to consider the potential benefits of relocating to communities with greater resources and opportunities.

Limited Social and Economic Mobility: In some cases, Black communities may face significant social and economic mobility barriers. These barriers can include limited job prospects, lower wages, restricted access to capital for entrepreneurship, and limited opportunities for upward mobility. When individuals and families are continuously trapped in cycles of poverty and limited prospects, strategic relocation to areas with greater economic opportunities and supportive environments may be a viable option for improving their circumstances.

Safety and Security Concerns: Safety and security are critical considerations when evaluating the sustainability of a community. Unfortunately, some Black communities face higher crime rates, increased violence, and inadequate law enforcement responses, leading to concerns for personal safety and well-being. When efforts to address these issues yield minimal results, individuals and families may need to prioritize their safety and consider relocation to communities with more robust safety measures and a supportive environment.

Diminished Educational Opportunities: Access to quality education is essential for individual and community success. However, many Black communities suffer from underfunded schools, limited resources, and disparities in educational outcomes. When educational opportunities are limited and hinder the prospects of future generations, families may opt to relocate to areas with better schools and educational support systems.

Environmental Hazards and Health Disparities: Black communities often face disproportionate exposure to environmental hazards, leading to adverse health outcomes. Factors such as proximity to industrial facilities, pollution, and limited access to healthcare contribute to health disparities within these communities. When efforts to mitigate these hazards and address health disparities are insufficient, individuals and families may prioritize their health and well-being by seeking communities with a healthier and more supportive environment.

Making the decision

The decision to relocate requires careful consideration and assessment of various factors. Here are some key points to evaluate:

1. Evaluate the availability of resources, such as infrastructure, economic opportunities, education, healthcare, and community services. Compare the resources in the current community with those in potential relocation destinations.
2. Consider the long-term prospects for individual and community growth and development. Assess the potential for upward mobility, economic advancement, and community sustainability.
3. Assess the safety and security of the current community, taking into account crime rates, law enforcement support, and personal safety concerns. Compare these factors with potential relocation destinations.
4. Evaluate the quality of the education system in the current community and potential relocation destinations. Consider the opportunities for educational advancement and the support available for children and youth.
5. Assess the environmental hazards and health disparities in the current community and consider potential relocation destinations that offer a healthier and safer environment.

6. Explore the presence of supportive networks and organizations that can aid in the transition to a new community. Consider the potential for social integration, cultural affinity, and access to community resources.

To where should we could we relocate?

There are several options and frames of thought concerning the strategic relocation of Black Communities. Charles Blow, the author of "The Devil You Know: A Black Power Manifesto," proposes that African Americans should consider reversing the Great Migration by concentrating in Southern states. He suggests that this migration could provide access to state power, enabling Black communities to transition from minority status to a super majority, thus wielding significant political and economic influence. Blow attributes the substantial growth of the Black population in Georgia to its ability to influence the state's political landscape, notably in the 2020 Elections.

I am inclined to support the idea that when Black communities find themselves in areas where they struggle to make meaningful advancements in their quality of life, a reverse migration could be a potential solution. However, it's important to note that failure to organize such a movement properly could lead to unintended consequences, potentially transferring the same unlivable anti-Black conditions from the North and West to the South. Furthermore, for this to be successful, specific communities may need to demonstrate and advertise themselves as places where Black people can develop and flourish. This type of claim would need to be backed with evidence of the ability to enact programs similar to those mentioned in the actions suggested.

Expatriation to Africa, particularly Ghana, has been suggested as a potential solution for African Americans seeking psychological liberation and a higher quality of life. While there are anecdotal testimonies of individuals experiencing a sense of liberation upon returning to Africa, it is crucial to approach this concept with a balanced perspective.

Firstly, there is no widespread evidence to suggest that a mass expatriation of African Americans to any location would automatically lead to the desired improvements in the quality of life for the entire community. Quality of life can vary significantly from one location to another, and many factors beyond geographical location contribute to individuals' well-being.

While several African nations have extended invitations to descendants in the diaspora to return, it is essential to note that living conditions in these nations, like in any country, can vary widely. While some individuals and families may find fulfillment and opportunities for personal and cultural connection, this experience may not be universal.

Furthermore, it is essential to consider that expatriation has been and continues to remain a complex and individual decision. While some African Americans have chosen to move to African countries, it is not a solution that will work for everyone. Various factors, including personal motivations, cultural ties, economic opportunities, and more, influence decisions to relocate.

The Ghanaian government has made efforts to facilitate the return of the African diaspora with initiatives like the 'Right of Abode' law and the establishment of a Diaspora Affairs Bureau. Responding to these efforts, at least 1,500 African Americans have relocated to Ghana since 2019. However, it is vital to approach expatriation as a personal choice and not as a one-size-fits-all solution for addressing systemic challenges faced by African Americans in the United States.

In summary, while expatriation to Africa is an option that some individuals and families may explore, it should be considered within the broader context of individual circumstances and preferences. It is not a singular solution for addressing the challenges faced by African Americans, and other approaches, such as community empowerment and systemic change, should also be explored and pursued.

It is crucial to approach the decision to relocate carefully, considering the unique circumstances and needs of individuals, families, and communities. While this is typically done at an individual and family level, these decisions may require community-wide inputs. When necessary, strategic relocation can provide opportunities for new beginnings, increased access to resources, and improved overall well-being.

Review: Building a Sustainable Future for Black America

This chapter offers a compelling and comprehensive set of community-level initiatives to address the challenges and disparities identified through the SWOT analysis. These initiatives reflect not only my dedication to addressing the enduring impacts of racism and White supremacy but also their practical experience in implementing similar programs across various communities.

Action 1 - Prioritizing Community Healing & Emotional Emancipation: It is crucial to recognize the importance of emotional well-being and healing. Addressing the historical trauma inflicted by racism and White supremacy is a necessary step towards community empowerment. Prioritizing mental and emotional health is essential for building resilience and fostering positive change.

Action 2 - Investing in Culturally Relevant Education: Investing in African-centered, culturally relevant, and anti-racist education for Black youth is paramount. It acknowledges the power of education in breaking cycles of inequality and bias. Providing students with an inclusive and empowering educational experience is key to shaping future leaders.

Action 3 - Cultivating Family Empowerment: Addressing cultural dysfunction by empowering families is commendable. It recognizes the pivotal role of family units in shaping communities and emphasizes the importance of fostering healthy relationships and values. Strengthening families can serve as a foundation for broader community transformation.

Action 4 - Using Cultural Policy for Building Social Capital: Incorporating cultural policy to build Black social capital is a strategic move. It acknowledges the significance of cultural expression and heritage in fostering unity and pride within the Black community. Such policies can help bridge cultural divides and promote a stronger sense of identity and belonging.

Action 5 - Community-Based Participatory Planning and Research: Utilizing community-based participatory planning and research to enhance social capital is empowering. It promotes collaboration between researchers and community members, ensuring that solutions are contextually relevant and community-driven. This approach can lead to sustainable social capital development.

Action 6 - Intentional Black Sustainability and Resilience: The proposal to foster sustainability and resilience in the face of global climate change is both forward-thinking and essential. It acknowledges the intersectionality of environmental justice and social equity, recognizing the disproportionate impact of climate change on marginalized communities. This action underscores the importance of adapting to environmental challenges and proactively addressing them.

Action 7 - Practicing Collective Civic Engagement: The proposal for collective civic engagement underscores the importance of political participation and advocacy. It encourages the Black community to actively shape policies and decisions that affect their lives. This action empowers individuals to make their voices heard and drive meaningful change.

Action 8 - Resisting Gentrification and Preventing Displacement: African American communities must develop multi-pronged strategies to resist serial forced displacement. In response to gentrification threats, proposed interventions include Community Land Trusts for perpetual community-owned land, economic empowerment through local businesses and cooperatives, cultural preservation efforts, affordable housing initiatives, legal advocacy, community education, and strategic collaborations. These measures aim to empower Black communities, preserve cultural heritage, and resist displacement.

Action 9 - Assessing the Need for Strategic Relocation: Strategic relocation is considered a pragmatic response to challenges faced by specific communities. It recognizes that, in some cases, relocation may offer better opportunities and resources. This action highlights the importance of assessing each community's unique needs and circumstances.

Conclusion

In this chapter, I set out to present a visionary roadmap for addressing the deep-seated issues facing Black communities in the United States. These initiatives, born from a combination of experience and a commitment to justice, offer a path toward empowerment, resilience, and equity. They are poised to demonstrate that intentional, community-driven efforts can disrupt the cycle of dysfunction and pave the way for a more sustainable and equitable future. This chapter serves as a call to action for individuals, organizations, and policymakers dedicated to creating positive social change.

10

From Dreams to Reality: Forging a Sustainable Future for Black Communities

"Dreams only a Dream if work don't follow it"
Kendrick Lamar

In the realm of community, the pursuit of sustainability extends far beyond the mere preservation of the environment. It demands a profound and all-encompassing approach that ensures the flourishing of Black communities in every facet of existence. We stand at a crossroads, for the sustainability of Black communities transcends the boundaries of physical freedom, mental well-being, and physical health. It is about ensuring that Black people develop social structures needed for their contemporary survival without compromising the well-being of future generations. This is a polarity to manage. Here is the catch: racism adds an extra layer of challenges to an already delicate situation. It further complicates our collective conundrum, making it even more crucial to take a holistic approach.

The Racism-Community Dysfunction Cycle is a complex and inter-related phenomenon that sustains the oppression experienced by Black communities. Breaking this cycle requires addressing both the social capital deficits caused by systemic racism and the cultural dysfunctions that reinforce harmful practices. This can be achieved through community development initiatives, educational programs, mentorship opportunities, and economic empowerment initiatives. Furthermore, by intentionally strengthening Black social capital, Black communities can better address common issues and achieve collective self-determination.

Addressing cultural dysfunctions requires a process of healing, empowerment, and transformation within the community. This involves fostering a sense of pride, self-worth, and collective identity among community members. This will not happen without the strategic and intentional promotion of dialogue, critical consciousness, and positive community norms that counteract the internalized oppression and distrust perpetuated by systemic racism. Creating community engagement, activism, and leadership development spaces is imperative to develop the necessary faith in Black people's collective self-efficacy.

The strategies highlighted in this book are intended to educate, engage, and mobilize community members while promoting collaboration, resilience, and sustainable progress. Through the implementation of locally tailored pragmatic programs and learning from historical and real-world examples, Black communities can prioritize their efforts and work towards tangible gains that accumulate into long-term progress. By leveraging strengths, capitalizing on opportunities, and building collaborative networks, communities can empower themselves and foster resilience in the face of challenges.

Throughout this journey, I have shared data from interviews, focus groups, and survey data from national data sets. These sources provide valuable insights into the contemporary realities we confront and the complex societal tapestry surrounding African Americans. The themes that emerged during my analysis capture some of our communities' most common strengths, weaknesses, opportunities, and threats. From this context, I churned out strategic approaches that allow the utilization of our strengths to reinforce our weak points and vulnerabilities and utilize our opportunities to mitigate threats.

From the voices of Black people, specific themes have emerged, such as shining stars in the night sky. They remind us of the importance of community engagement, the need to address the root causes of crime, the power of building social capital, the relentless fight against racism, and the call for environmental justice. Our fellow community members have shared their stories, shedding light on what matters most in our collective existence. They have sounded the alarms for active participation, education, and cooperation. They have exposed the limitations of existing systems and urged us to tackle public health, poverty, and the well-being of our planet head-on.

But we must face the facts about the political landscape in our country and our planet. We recognize that racism and White supremacy are woven into the fabric of the United States. Removing these elements would ultimately require a comprehensive transformation of what it means to be American. Thus, we will face backlash, a storm of oppressive forces, and anti-democratic sentiments. This is a harsh reminder that we must relentlessly face our better-prepared opponents, knowing that we may not see any immediate benefits from our efforts. Yet, and still, we can not afford to sit back and let the cycle continue.

This means that Black organizations must reclaim our narrative and rewrite our story with a theme of Black Sustainability as our guiding principle. The survival of future generations of Black people requires us now to successfully reshape our communities, not as passive bystanders but as architects of change. Find ways to build trust, foster civic engagement, and strengthen social networks in Black America. Through unity and organization, Black communities can produce resilient warriors for progress and champions of Black sustainability.

We cannot separate the fight against racism and oppression from the struggle for environmental justice. That's why we must push back against those who dismiss diversity, equity, and inclusion efforts. These elements are critical for establishing an effective democracy. We can not settle for shallow progress or half-hearted attempts to address the deep-rooted injustices plaguing us. We have to remain aware of the legacies of slavery, discrimination, and disenfranchisement that continue to shape our present. Only through this intentional awareness can we break the chains of psychological oppression and pursue a future that honors our ancestors' struggles.

Prerequisites for Progress

Black communities must establish a strong foundation on several critical elements to achieve meaningful and lasting progress. No one strategic approach will have a meaningful impact without these prerequisite conditions. These elements are not optional—they are essential pillars determining Black communities' future sustainability and resilience.

First and foremost, it is imperative that Black people recognize the immense cultural, economic, and political value they bring to the U.S. and the world. We must see our Blackness as a valuable asset integral to humanity's survival. This self-recognition is vital, regardless of whether others acknowledge it. It must be internalized as a source of strength, motivation, and purpose.

Also, Black solidarity is a non-negotiable requirement for progress, but true unity requires us first to address internal barriers. Inclusivity within the Black community is crucial. We must embrace our diversity —whether it be differences in class, gender, or experiences. Failing to recognize and honor the full spectrum of Black identity weakens the community from within. It leaves us all vulnerable to divide-and-conquer tactics regularly employed by our oppressors. Thus, class consciousness is a crucial component to building black solidarity and understanding the shared struggles of Black working-class and middle-class individuals. Furthermore, gender power parity ensures that Black women have equal leadership, influence, and opportunity. Without embracing these critical factors, achieving adequate levels of solidarity is unlikely.

Ultimately, progress requires a comprehensive intentional purge of internalized racism and rejection of white supremacy. These remnants of oppressive systems manifest as self-doubt, competition, and division within the community. Actual progress requires the outright mass rejection of these ideologies and a consistent effort to heal the wounds inflicted. I say this to say that overcoming external racism is vital, but cleansing our minds and communities of its toxic residue is tantamount.

There is also a desperate need for political maturity in Black American communities. Black communities must become deeply engaged in shaping policies that affect their lives. This includes voting and advocating for policies prioritizing Black interests, running for office, and holding elected officials accountable. It is of the utmost importance that our political strategy is not confined to a partisan apparatus. However, this is not a call for a break from our current coalition within the Democratic party; however, the terms of this alliance should be routinely negotiated to ensure that Black interests are prioritized. Organized and informed civic engagement is necessary to build Black political power. Political power is a tool for systemic change, and without it, Black communities will remain vulnerable to the whims of a system not designed to serve them.

It is also essential to recognize the value of social trust. Social trust is an invaluable currency enabling communities to effectively address collective challenges. It is the foundation for cooperation, collaboration, and mutual support, fostering a sense of unity and shared purpose. Without social trust, Black communities will continue to struggle to mobilize for change, as mistrust renders them vulnerable to divisive tactics from their opponents to undermine their efforts to tackle shared problems.

Finally, there must be a shared commitment to intentional action. This is not a passive journey. Black communities must unify with a clear, deliberate focus on sustaining their future. This means working collectively to build social, economic, and political structures that support long-term growth and stability. Intentionality is of the utmost importance—it is not enough to hope for change; we must plan for it, work toward it, and ensure that each action contributes to the well-being of future generations.

Waking Up

To be woke means to be an agent of change, a vessel of consciousness, and a guardian against oppression. Being "woke" requires painful sacrifice, but those who remain asleep are pawns in a game of power. So, I urge those who agree to wake up from those nightmares of indifference and complacency. Put aside petty differences that pale in comparison to the importance of our collective success.

By standing together, we increase our ability to dismantle the systems that seek to diminish our humanity. This will allow us to nurture vibrant communities that thrive with life and interconnectedness. The future of our communities depends on the bonds of trust, civic engagement, and collective action that we build today. Only in a unified front can we eliminate many of our most significant vulnerabilities, but this requires that we remove our internalized White supremacy from hearts, minds, and souls and unite under the banner of justice. A unified Black community is among humanity's greatest chance to save it from the White supremacist patriarchy that is destroying the planet. This is the heart of our modern-day human rights movement. So, let's sow the seeds of progress so future generations of African people can thrive.

The world's political forecast may seem gloomy, overshadowed by environmental destruction, greed, racism, class warfare, and anti-democratic forces. However, our ancestors serve as examples of our people's ingenuity in surmounting the most perilous obstacles. We can use their stories as inspiration to confront injustice and oppression and push forward with unwavering resolve. Our struggle for the planet is intrinsically linked to the fight for justice, equity, and liberation.

In the spirit of all our ancestors, known and unknown, who sacrificed and prayed for our existence, let's be the vanguards of progress, the drum majors of justice, and the torchbearers of a new era that allows our descendants to inherit a viable planet. With every ounce of our collective being, we declare, by any dreams necessary, that we will forge a sustainable future for Black communities, where freedom and justice are not abstract notions but a daily reality for African people.

So, the time for writing is over! Think of this work like an alarm clock. Wake up! It's time to get back to work. It's time to reorganize, reeducate, and be the change that leads our people toward a future of Black sustainability. Together, we will continue converting our ancestors' dreams to our descendants' reality.

References

Abbott, S. (2009). Social capital and health: The problematic roles of social networks and social surveys. *Health Sociology Review, 18*(3), 297-306. Retrieved from http://openaccess.city.ac.uk/id/eprint/463.

Abrams, L. S., & Molo, J. A. (2009). Critical race theory and the cultural competence dilemma in social work education. *Journal of Social Work Education, 45*(2), 245-261. https://doi.org/10.5175/JSWE.2009.200700109.

Adger, W. N. (2003). Social capital, collective action and adaptation to climate change. *Economic Geography, 79*(4), 387-404.

Alaimo, K., Reischl, T. M., & Allen, J. O. (2010). Community gardening, neighborhood meetings and social capital. *Journal of Community Psychology, 38*(4), 497-514. https://doi.org/10.1002/jcop.20378.

Aldrich, D. P. (2012). *Building resilience: Social capital in post-disaster recovery*. University of Chicago Press.

Aldrich, D. P., & Meyer, M. A. (2015). Social capital and community resilience. *Community Resilience Theory, 59*(2), 254-269.

Alexander, M. (2012). *The new Jim Crow*. The New Press.

Asabor, E. N., Lett, E., Mosely, B., Boone, C. A., Sundaresan, S., Wong, T. A., Majumder, M. S., & others. (2023). A mixed-methods assessment of off-duty police shootings in a media-curated database. *Health Services Research*. https://doi.org/10.1111/1475-6773.14170

Baik, S., Crittenden, J., & Coleman, R. (2023). Social capital and formal volunteering among family and unpaid caregivers of older adults. *Research on Aging*.

Benet, W. J. (2006). *The polarity management model of workplace democracy* (Doctoral dissertation, Ontario Institute for Studies in Education of the University of Toronto, Canada). Retrieved from ProQuest Dissertations & Theses Full Text database, UMI Publishing. (Order No. NR15724).

Benet, W. (2012a). Managing the polarities of democracy: A social econony framework for healthy, sustainable, and just communities. Retrieved from http://socialeconomics.org/Papers/Benet6A.pdf

Benet, W. (2012b). *The polarities of democracy: A theoretical framework for building a healthy, sustainable, and just world.* Unpublished Manuscript. Social Economy Centre, Adult Education and Community Development Program of the University of Toronto, Canada.

Benet, W. (2013). Managing the polarities of democracy: A theoretical framework for positive social change. *Journal of Social Change, 5*(1), 26-39. doi:10.5590/JOSC.2013.05.1.03

Bergstrand, K., Mayer, B., Brumback, B., & Zhang, Y. (2015). Assessing the relationship between social vulnerability and community resilience to hazards. *Social Indicator Research, 122,* 391-409.

BlackDemographics.com. (2023). Employment. Retrieved June 7, 2024, from https://blackdemographics.com/economics/employment/

Blair, J. P., & Carroll, M. C. (2008). Social capital. *Economic Development Journal, 7*(3), 42-49. Retrieved from http://web.cued.org/EDJournal/Summer_08/IEDC_EDJ_Blair.pdf.

Borman, K. E., Eitle, T. M., Michael, D., Eitle, D. J., Lee, R., Johnson, L., Shircliffe, B. (2004). Accountability in a post-desegregation era: The continuing significance of segregation in Florida's schools. *American Educational Research Journal, 41*(3), 605-631. Retrieved from http://www.jstor.org/stable/3699440.

Boston, P. Q., Strouble, B. W., Balogun, A., Lugo-Martinez, B., McClain, M., Mitchell, M. M., ... Garibay, C. (2023). Community voices on the experiences of community-based participatory research in the environmental justice movement. *Social Sciences, 12*(6), 358.

Bourdieu, P. (1986). The forms of capital. In J. Richardson (Ed.), *Handbook of Theory and Research for the Sociology of Education* (pp. 241-258). Greenwood Press.

Brondolo, E., Libretti, M., Riviera, L., & Walsemann, K. M. (2012). Racism and social capital: The implications for social and physical well-being. *Journal of Social Issues, 68*(2), 358-384. https://doi.org/10.1111/j.1540-4560.2012.01752.x.

Brondolo, E., Love, E. E., Pencille, M., Shoenthaler, A., & Ogedegbe, G. (2011). Racism and hypertension: A review of the empirical evidence and implications for clinical practice. *American Journal of Hypertension, 24*(5), 518-529. https://doi.org/10.1038/ajh.2011.9

Broska, L. H. (2021). It's all about community: On the interplay of social capital, social needs, and environmental concern in sustainable community action. *Energy Research & Social Science, 79,* 102-111. https://doi.org/10.1016/j.erss.2021.102111.

Brown, E., & Ferris, J. M. (2007). Social capital and philanthropy: An analysis of the impact of social capital on individual giving and volunteering. *Nonprofit and Voluntary Sector Quarterly, 36*(1), 85-99. https://doi.org/10.1177/0899764006293178.

Bureau of Labor Statistics. (2024). Table A-2. Employment status of the civilian population by race, sex, and age. Retrieved from https://www.bls.gov/news.release/empsit.t02.htm

Carson, C., Lapsansky-Werner, E. J., & Nash, G. B. (2018). *The struggle for freedom: A history of African Americans, combined volume* (3rd ed.). Pearson.

Chiesi, A. M. (2007). Measuring social capital and its effectiveness: The case of small entrepreneurs in Italy. *European Sociological Review, 23*(4), 467-481. https://doi.org/10.1093/esr/jcm010.

Coleman, J. S. (1988). Social capital in the creation of human capital. *American Journal of Sociology, 94*(S1), S95-S120. https://doi.org/10.1086/228943.

Collins, C. A., & Williams, D. R. (1999). Segregation and mortality: The deadly effects of racism. *Sociological Forum, 14*(3), 495-523. Retrieved from http://download.springer.com/static/pdf/106/art%253A10.1023%252FA%253A021403820451.pdf?auth66=1394311285_bb9ef82d97bd3ce629cfb768c7465aed&ext=.pdf.

Collins, C., Asante-Muhammad, D., Hoxie, J., & Nieves, E. (2017). *The road to zero wealth: How the racial wealth divide is hollowing out America's middle class.* Institute for Policy Studies and Prosperity Now.

Collins, C., Asante-Muhammed, D., Hoxie, J., & Terry, S. (2019). *Dreams deferred: How enriching the 1% widens the racial wealth divide.* Institute for Policy Studies.

Cook, D. A., & Dixon, A. D. (2013). Writing critical race theory and method: A composite counterstory on the experiences of Black teachers in New Orleans post-Katrina. *International Journal of Qualitative Studies in Education, 26*(10), 1238-1258. https://doi.org/10.1080/09518398.2012.731531.

Cornwell, E. Y., & Cornwell, B. (2008). Access to expertise as a form of social capital: An examination of race- and class-based disparities in network ties to experts. *Sociological Perspectives, 51*(4), 853-876. https://doi.org/10.1525/sop.2008.51.4.853.

Dixson, A. D., & Rousseau, C. K. (2005). And we still are not saved: Critical race theory in education ten years later. *Race Ethnicity and Education, 8*(1), 7-27. https://doi.org/10.1080/1361332052000340971

Douglass, D., & Browne, A. (2011). Surviving the downturn: The role of social capital in the financial crisis. *The Western Journal of Black Studies, 35*(2), 128+.

Downey, L., & Hawkins, B. (2008). Race, income, and environmental inequality in the United States. *Sociological Perspectives, 51*(4), 759-781. https://doi.org/10.1525/sop.2008.51.4.759.

Du Bois, W. E. B. (1935, October 1). Inter-racial implications of the Ethiopian crisis: A Negro view. *The Crisis.*

Eisenman, D. P., Adams, R. M., & Rivard, H. (2016). Measuring outcomes in a community resilience program: A new metric for evaluation results at the household level. *PLOS Currents Disasters, 8.* https://doi.org/10.1371/currents.dis.16c5b9e7d88e1db67d5aeca90e61e531

Eisenman, D., Chandra, A., Fogleman, S., Magana, A., Hendricks, A., Wells, K., ... Plough, A. (2014). The Los Angeles County community disaster resilience project: A community-level, public health initiative to build community disaster resilience. *International Journal of Environmental Research and Public Health, 11*(8), 8475-8490. https://doi.org/10.3390/ijerph110808475

Fitzpatrick, K. M., Piko, B. F., Wright, D. R., & LaGory, M. (2005). Depressive symptomatology, exposure to violence, and the role of social capital among African American adolescents. *American Journal of Orthopsychiatry, 75*(2), 262-274. https://doi.org/10.1037/0002-9432.75.2.262

Florida, R., & Mellander, C. (2015). *Segregated city: The geography of economic segregation in America's metros.* Martin Prosperity Institute.

Folland, S. (2007). Does "community social capital" contribute to population health? *Social Science & Medicine, 64*(1), 2342-2354. https://doi.org/10.1016/j.socscimed.2007.03.003.

Fraser, T., Aldrich, D. P., & Page-Tan, C. (2021). Bowling alone or distancing together? The role of social capital in excess death rates from COVID-19. *Social Science & Medicine, 284*, 114241. https://doi.org/10.1016/j.socscimed.2021.114241

Fullilove, M. T. (2016). *Root shock: How tearing up city neighborhoods hurts America, and what we can do about it.* New Village Press.

Gawronski, B., Peters, K. R., & Brochu, P. M. (2008). Understanding the relations between different forms of racial prejudice: A cognitive consistency perspective. *Personality and Social Psychology Bulletin, 34*(5), 648-665. https://doi.org/10.1177/0146167207313729.

Giacovelli, G. (2022). Social capital and energy transition: A conceptual review. *Energy in the 21st Century: Prospects and Sustainability, 14*(15).

Gilbert, K. L., Ransome, Y., Dean, L. T., DeCaille, J., & Kawachi, I. (2022). Social capital, Black social mobility, and health disparities. *Annual Review of Public Health, 43*, 173-191.

Gilbert, K., & Dean, L. (2013). Social capital, social policy and health disparities: A legacy of political advocacy in African American communities. In I. Kawachi, S. Takao, & S. V. Subramanian (Eds.), *Global perspectives on social capital* (pp. 307-322). Springer. https://doi.org/10.1007/978-1-4614-7464-7.

Gil-Rivas, V., & Kilmer, R. (2016). Building community capacity and fostering disaster resilience. *Journal of Clinical Psychology, 72*(12), 1318-1332. https://doi.org/10.1002/jclp.22327

Glaeser, E., & Vigdor, J. (2012). *The end of the segregated century: Racial separation in America's neighborhoods, 1890-2010.* Manhattan Institute for Policy Research. Retrieved from https://www.manhattan-institute.org/html/cr_66.htm.

Graddy, E., & Wang, L. (2009). Community foundation development and social capital. *Nonprofit and Voluntary Sector Quarterly, 38*(3), 392-412. https://doi.org/10.1177/0899764008318609.

Graham, L., Brown-Jeffy, S., Aronson, R., & Stephens, C. (2011). Critical race theory as theoretical framework and analysis tool for population health research. *Critical Public Health, 21*(1), 81-93. https://doi.org/10.1080/09581596.2010.493173.

Green, P. C. (2008). The impact of law on African American males. *American Behavioral Scientist, 51*(7), 872-884. https://doi.org/10.1177/0002764207311995.

Greenbaum, S. (2008). Poverty and the willful destruction of social capital: Displacement and dispossession in African American communities. *Rethinking Marxism, 20*(1), 43-55. https://doi.org/10.1080/08935690701739956.

Griffith, D. M., Johnson, J., Ellis, K. R., & Schulz, A. J. (2010). Cultural context: A critical approach to eliminating health disparities. *Ethnicity & Disease, 20*(1), 71-76. Retrieved from http://www.ishib.org/ED/journal/20-1/ethn-20-01-71.pdf.

Grootaert, C., & Bastelaer, T. V. (2002). *Understanding and measuring social capital: A multidisciplinary tool for practitioners.* The World Bank.

Hampton, L. A., & Duncan, E. M. (2011). Identities and inequalities: An examination of the role of racial identity inside a voluntary youth organization. *Social Identities, 17*(4), 477-500. https://doi.org/10.1080/13504630.2011.587303.

Haney-Lopez, I. F. (2010). Post racial racism: Racial stratification and mass incarceration in the age of Obama. *California Law Review, 98*(3), 1023-1073. Retrieved from http://scholarship.law.berkeley.edu/californialawreview.

Hanifan, L. (1916). The rural school community center. *Annals of the American Academy of Political and Social Science, 67*, 130-138. Retrieved from http://www.jstor.org/stable/1013498.

Hardaway, C. R., & McLoyd, V. C. (2009). Escaping poverty and securing middle class status: How race and socioeconomic status shape mobility prospects for African Americans during the transition to adulthood. *Journal of Youth and Adolescence, 38*(2), 242-256. https://doi.org/10.1007/s10964-008-9354-z.

Harris, A. P. (2012). Critical race theory. University of California, Davis. Retrieved from http://works.bepress.com/angela_harris/17.

Hawkins, R. L., & Maurer, K. (2010). Bonding, bridging and linking: How social capital operated in New Orleans following Hurricane Katrina. *British Journal of Social Work, 40*(6), 1777-1793. https://doi.org/10.1093/bjsw/bcp087.

Henkel, K. E., Dovidio, J. F., & Gaertner, S. L. (2006). Institutional discrimination, individual racism and Hurricane Katrina. *Analyses of Social Issues and Public Policy, 6*(1), 99-124. https://doi.org/10.1111/j.1530-2415.2006.00106.x.

Hero, R. E. (2007). *Racial diversity and social capital.* Cambridge University Press.

Hipolito-Delgado, C. P. (2010). Exploring the etiology of ethnic self-hatred: Internalized racism in Chicana/o and Latina/o college students. *Journal of College Student Development, 51*(3), 319-331. https://doi.org/10.1353/csd.0.0133.

Hobson-Prater, T., & Leech, T. (2012). The significance of race for neighborhood social cohesion: Perceived difficulty of collection action in majority Black neighborhoods. *Journal of Sociology and Social Welfare, 39*(1), 89-109.

Holloway, K. (2021, November 1). How thousands of Black farmers were forced off their land. *The Nation.* https://www.thenation.com/article/society/black-farmers-pigford-debt/

Huddy, L., & Feldman, S. (2009). On assessing the political effects of racial prejudice. *Annual Review of Political Science, 12,* 423-447. https://doi.org/10.1146/annurev.polisci.11.062906.070752.

Hudson, L., & Chapman, C. (2002, September). The measurement of social capital in the United States. *International Conference on the Measurement of Social Capital* (pp. 1-14). London. Retrieved from http://www.oecd.org/unitedstates/2382454.pdf.

Hutchinson, R. N., Putt, M. A., Dean, L. T., Long, J. A., & Montagnet, C. A. (2009). Neighborhood racial composition, social capital and Black all-cause mortality in Philadelphia. *Social Science & Medicine, 68*(10), 1859-1865. https://doi.org/10.1016/j.socscimed.2009.02.005.

Hylton, K. (2010). How a turn to critical race theory can contribute to our understanding of race, racism and anti-racism in sport. *International Review for the Sociology of Sport, 45*(3), 335-354. https://doi.org/10.1177/1012690210371045.

Hyyppa, M. T. (2010). *Healthy ties: Social capital, population health, and survival.* Springer.

Israel, B. A., Coombe, C. M., & McGranaghan, R. (2009). Community-based participatory research: A participatory approach for public health. Retrieved from Michigan Public Health Training Center: www.cbpr-training.org.

Jackson-Lowman, H. (2020). Serial forced displacements and the decline of Ubuntu in Afrikan American communities. *Alternation, 27*(1), 153-169.

Jackson-Lowman, H., & Haile, B. (2014). The missing tool in the development of Black community agency and empowerment. *Black Child Journal, 2*(1), 64-75.

Jacques, P. J., Broad, K., Butler, W., Emrich, C., Galindao, S., Knox, C., ... Ziewitz, K. (2017). Human dimensions and communication of Florida's climate. In E. P. Chassignet, J. W. Jones, M. Vasubandhy, & J. Obeysekera (Eds.), *Florida's climate: Changes variations and impacts* (pp. 1-50). Florida Climate Institute.

Johnson, B. (1996). *Polarity management: Identifying and managing unsolvable problems.* HRD Press, Inc.

Johnson, C. A. (2011). How do public libraries create social capital? An analysis of interactions between library staff and patrons. *Library & Information Science Research, 34*(1), 52-62. https://doi.org/10.1016/j.lisr.2011.07.009.

Johnson, N. L., Suarez, R., & Lundy, M. (2003). The importance of social capital in Colombian rural agro-enterprises. *Proceedings of the 25th Conference of Agricultural Economist* (pp. 1152-1158). Document Transformation Technologies. Retrieved from http://www.ifpri.org/publication/importance-social-capital-colombian-rural-agro-enterprises.

Johnson, C. O., Boon-Dooley, A. S., DeCleene, N. K., Henny, K. F., Blacker, B. F., Anderson, J. A., Afshin, A., Aravkin, A., Cunningham, M. W., Dieleman, J. L., Feldman, R. G., Gakidou, E., Mokdad, A. H., Naghavi, M., Spencer, C. N., Whisnant, J. L., York, H. W., Zende, R. R., Zheng, P., Murray, C. J. L., & Roth, G. A. (2022). Life expectancy for White, Black, and Hispanic race/ethnicity in U.S. states: Trends and disparities, 1990 to 2019. *Annals of Internal Medicine, 175*(8), 1031-1041. https://doi.org/10.7326/M21-3956.

Jones, C. P. (2002). Confronting institutionalized racism. *Phylon, 50*(1/2), 7-22. Retrieved December 25, 2012, from http://www.jstor.org/stable/4149999.

Jordan, J. (2014). Swimming alone? The role of social capital in enhancing local resilience to climate stress: A case study from Bangladesh. *Climate and Development, 6*(2), 110-123. https://doi.org/10.1080/17565529.2014.886994.

Jbaily, A., Zhou, X., Liu, J., Lee, T.-H., Kamareddine, L., Verguet, S., & Dominici, F. (2022). Air pollution exposure disparities across U.S. population and income groups. *Nature, 601*(7893), 228-233. https://doi.org/10.1038/s41586-021-04190-y.

Kang, J., & Lane, K. (2010). Seeing through colorblindness: Implicit bias and the law. *UCLA Law Review, 58*(2), 465-520. Retrieved from http://uclalawreview.org/pdf/58-2-3.pdf.

Kelly, B. P. (2012). Social capital in the lives of young adult African American male achievers (Doctoral dissertation, Walden University). Available from ProQuest Dissertations and Theses database. (UMI No. 3494466).

Kennedy, R. L. (1989). Racial critiques of legal academia. *Harvard Law Review, 102*(8), 1745-1819. Retrieved from www.jstor.org/stable/1341357.

Kim, N., & Shim, C. (2018). Social capital, knowledge sharing and innovation of small- and medium-sized enterprises in a tourism cluster. *International Journal of Contemporary Hospitality Management, 30*(5), 2050-2069.

King, M. B. (2006). A Black/non-Black theory of African-American partisanship hostility, consciousness and the Republican Party (Doctoral dissertation). University of North Texas.

Kitchen, P., & Williams, A. (2012). Measuring social capital in Hamilton, Ontario. *Social Indicators Research, 108*(1), 215-238. https://doi.org/10.1007/s11205-012-006-3.

Kochar, R., Fry, R., & Taylor, P. (2011). Wealth gaps rise to record highs between Whites, Blacks, and Hispanics. *Social & Demographic Trends.* Retrieved November

7, 2013, from http://www.pewsocialtrends.org/2011/07/26/wealth-gaps-rise-to-record-highs-between-whites-blacks-hispanics/.

Krasny, M. E., Kalbacker, L., Stedman, R. C., & Russ, A. (2013). Measuring social capital among youth: Applications in environmental education. *Environmental Education Research, 21*(1), 1-22. https://doi.org/10.1080/13504622.2013.843647.

Krishna, A., & Shrader, E. (2002). The social capital assessment tool: Design and implementation. In C. Grootaert, & B. T. Van (Eds.), *Understanding and measuring social capital* (pp. 17-40). The World Bank.

Krosch, A. R., & Amodio, D. M. (2014). Economic scarcity alters the perception of race. *Proceedings of the National Academy of Sciences, 111*(25), 9079-9084. https://doi.org/10.1073/pnas.1404448111.

Ladson-Billings, G. (2011). Race… to the top, again: Comments on the genealogy of critical race theory. *Connecticut Law Review, 43*(5), 1439-1457. Retrieved from http://archive.connecticutlawreview.org/documents/Billings.pdf.

Lane, H. M., Morello-Frosch, R., Marshall, J. D., & Apte, J. S. (2022). Historical redlining is associated with present-day air pollution disparities in U.S. cities. *Environmental Science & Technology Letters, 9*(4), 345-350. https://doi.org/10.1021/acs.estlett.1c01012.

Laurence, J. (2009). The effect of ethnic diversity and community disadvantage on social cohesion: A multi-level analysis of social capital and interethnic relations in UK communities. *European Sociological Review, 27*(1), 70-89. https://doi.org/10.1093/esr/jcp057.

Leichenko, R. (2011). Climate change and urban resilience. *Current Opinion in Environmental Sustainability, 3*(3), 164-168. https://doi.org/10.1016/j.cosust.2010.12.002.

Leppart, R. (2023, September). A look at Black-owned businesses in the U.S. *Pew Research Center*. Retrieved from https://pewrsr.ch/49jhYVy.

Letki, N. (2008). Does diversity erode social cohesion? Social capital and race in British neighborhoods. *Political Studies, 56*(1), 99-126. https://doi.org/10.1111/j.1467-9248.2007.00692.x.

Lewin, A., Mitchell, S. J., Rasmussen, A., Sanders-Phillips, K., & Joseph, J. G. (2011). Do human and social capital protect young African American mothers from depression associated with ethnic discrimination and violence exposure. *Journal of Black Psychology, 37*(3), 286-310. https://doi.org/10.1177/0095798410381242.

Leykin, D., Lahad, M., Cohen, O., Goldberg, A., & Aharonson-Daniel, L. (2013). Conjoint community resiliency assessment measure-28/10 items (CCRAM28 and CCRAM10): A self-report tool for assessing community resilience. *American Journal of Community Psychology, 52*(3-4), 313-323. https://doi.org/10.1007/s10464-013-9603-9.

Limbert, W. M., & Bullock, H. E. (2005). 'Playing the fool': US welfare policy from a critical race perspective. *Feminism & Psychology, 15*(3), 253-276. https://doi.org/10.1177/0959-353505054715.

Lin, N. (2000). Inequality in social capital. *Contemporary Sociology, 29*(6), 785-794. Retrieved from www.students.uni-mainz.de/bonea001/.../nan-lin-inequality-sc.pd.

Lin, N. (2008). A network theory of social capital. In D. Castiglione, J. W. van Deth, & G. Wolleb (Eds.), *The handbook of social capital* (pp. 50-69). Oxford University Press.

Liu, B., Austin, S. D., & Orey, B. D. (2009). Church attendance, social capital, and Black voting participation. *Social Science Quarterly, 90*(3), 566-592. https://doi.org/10.1111/j.1540-6237.2009.00632.x.

Logan, J. (2013). The persistence of segregation in the 21st century metropolis. *City & Community, 12*(2), 160-168. https://doi.org/10.1111/cico.12021.

Lopez, M. H., & Moslimani, M. (2023, February 10). Key facts about the nation's 47.2 million Black Americans. *Pew Research Center.* Retrieved from https://www.pewresearch.org/short-reads/2023/02/10/key-facts-about-black-americans/.

Luks, S., & Elms, L. (2005). African-American partisanship and the legacy of the civil rights movement: Generational, regional, and economic influences on Democratic identification, 1973-1994. *Political Psychology: Symposium: Race and Politics, 26*(5), 735-754.

Lynch, M. (2011). Crack pipes and policing: A case study of institutional racism and remedial action in Cleveland. *Law & Policy, 33*(2), 179-214.

McKenzie, B. D. (2008). Reconsidering the effects of bonding social capital: A closer look at Black civil society institutions in America. *Political Behavior, 30*(1), 25-45. https://doi.org/10.1007/s11109-007-9038-5.

McKenzie, S. (2004). *Social sustainability: Toward some definitions* (Hawke Research Institute Working Paper Series, No. 27). Retrieved from https://atn.edu.au/Documents/EASS/HRI/working-papers/wp27.pdf.

Meerow, S., Newell, J. P., & Stults, M. (2016). Defining urban resilience: A review. *Landscape and Urban Planning, 147*, 38-49. https://doi.org/10.1016/j.landurbplan.2015.11.011.

Mendez, D. D., Hogan, V. K., & Culhane, J. F. (2013). Stress during pregnancy: The role of institutional racism. *Stress Health, 29*(4), 266-274. https://doi.org/10.1002/smi.2462.

Menka, B., & Ryan, R. (2012). Influence of social capital on community preparedness for wildfires. *Landscape and Urban Planning, 106*(3), 253-261.

Meyer, M. A. (2016). Elderly perceptions of social capital and age-related disaster vulnerability. *Disaster Medicine and Public Health Preparedness, 11*(1), 48-55. https://doi.org/10.1017/dmp.2016.128.

Milner, R. H. (2013). Analyzing poverty, learning, and teaching through a critical race theory lens. *Review of Research in Education, 37*(1), 1-53. https://doi.org/10.3102/0091732X12459720.

Mohai, P., & Saha, R. (2007). Racial inequality in the distribution of hazardous waste: A national-level reassessment. *Social Problems, 54*(3), 343-379. https://doi.org/10.1525/sp.2007.54.3.343.

Moslimani, M., Tamir, C., Budiman, A., Noe-Bustamante, L., & Mora, L. (2024, January 18). Facts about the U.S. Black population. *Pew Research Center.*

Mohnen, S. M., Groenewegen, P. P., Volker, B., & Flap, H. (2011). Neighborhood social capital and individual health. *Social Science & Medicine, 72*(4), 660-667. https://doi.org/10.1016/j.socscimed.2010.12.004.

Moore, S., Daniel, M., Gauvin, L., & Dube, L. (2009). Not all social capital is good capital. *Health & Place, 15*(4), 1071-1077. https://doi.org/10.1016/j.healthplace.2009.05.005.

Murji, K. (2007). Sociological engagements: Institutional racism and beyond. *Sociology, 41*(5), 843-855. https://doi.org/10.1177/0038038507080440.

Murray, L., Njoku, N., & Davis, R. (2022). Greater funding, greater needs: A report on funding for HBCUs. Washington, DC: UNCF. Retrieved from https://www.luminafoundation.org/wp-content/uploads/2022/08/greater-funding-greater-needs-hbcus.pdf.

Mutawally, S. A. (2018). Social capital and academic achievement of African American male high school students (Doctoral dissertation). Walden University.

National Center for Education Statistics. (2017). Characteristics of public elementary and secondary school teachers in the United States: Results from the 2015–16 National Teacher and Principal Survey. Retrieved from https://nces.ed.gov/pubsearch/pubsinfo.asp?pubid=2017072.

National Center for Education Statistics. (2024). Private school enrollment: Last updated May 2024. Retrieved from https://nces.ed.gov/programs/digest/d23/tables/dt23_302.20.asp.

Nembhard, J. G. (2014). *Collective courage: A history of African American cooperative economic thought and practice.* Penn State University Press.

Newman, L. (2010). Social capital: A necessary and sufficient condition for sustainable community development? *Community Development Journal, 46*(1), 5-21. https://doi.org/10.1093/cdj/bsn028.

Nieminen, T., Martelin, T., Koskinen, S., Aro, H., Alanen, E., & Hyyppa, M. T. (2010). Social capital as a determinant of self-rated health and psychological well-being. *International Journal of Public Health, 55*(6), 531-542. https://doi.org/10.1007/s00038-010-0138-3.

Norton, M. I., & Sommers, S. R. (2011). Whites see racism as a zero-sum game that they are now losing. *Perspectives on Psychological Science, 6*(3), 215-220. https://doi.org/10.1177/1745691611406922.

Ndugga, N., & Artiga, S. (2023, February 13). How recognizing health disparities for Black people is important for change. *KFF.* https://www.kff.org/policy-watch/how-recognizing-health-disparities-for-black-people-is-important-for-change/

Oliver, M. L., & Shapiro, T. M. (2006). *Black wealth white wealth: A new perspective on racial inequality* (2nd ed.). Taylor & Francis Group.

Ornelas, I. J., Arnell, J., Tran, A. N., Royster, M., Armstrong-Brown, J., & Eng, E. (2009). Understanding African American men's perceptions of racism, male gender socialization, and social capital through Photovoice. *Qualitative Health Research, 19*(4), 552-565. https://doi.org/10.1177/1049732309332104.

Orr, M. (1999). *Black social capital: The politics of school reform in Baltimore 1986-1998.* University Press of Kansas.

Ortiz, L., & Jayshree, J. (2010). Critical race theory: A transformational model for teaching diversity. *Journal of Social Work Education, 46*(2), 175-193. https://doi.org/10.5175/JSWE.2010.20090070.

Ortiz, P. (2005). *Emancipation betrayed: The hidden history of Black organizing and white violence in Florida from reconstruction to the bloody election of 1920.* University of California Press.

Palmer, R. T. (2010). The impact of social capital on promoting the success of African American faculty. In S. E. Moore, R. Alexander Jr., & A. J. Lemelle Jr. (Eds.), *Dilemmas of Black faculty at U.S. predominantly white institutions: Issues in the post-multicultural era.* The Edwin Mellen Press. Retrieved from http://works.bepress.com/robert_palmer/12.

Palmer, R., & Gasman, M. (2008). "It takes a village to raise a child": The role of social capital in promoting academic success for African American men at a Black college. *Journal of College Student Development, 49*(1), 52-70. https://doi.org/10.1353/csd.2008.0002.

Parks, G. S. (2008). Toward a critical race realism. *Cornell Journal of Law and Public Policy, 17*(3), 683-745. Retrieved from http://www.gregoryparks.net/articles/1284849609CRR.pdf.

Pattillo, M. (2005). Black middle class neighborhoods. *Annual Review of Sociology, 31*(1), 305-329. https://doi.org/10.1146/annurev.soc.29.010202.095956.

Patton, M. Q. (2002). *Qualitative research and evaluation methods* (3rd ed.). Sage Publications, Inc.

Pearson, A. R., Dovidio, J. F., & Gaertner, S. L. (2009). The nature of contemporary prejudice: Insights from aversive racism. *Social and Personality Psychology Compass, 3*(3), 1-25. https://doi.org/10.1111/j.1751-9004.2009.00183.x.

Peek, R. (1965). Curbing voter intimidation in Florida: 1871. *The Florida Historical Quarterly, 43*(4), 333-348. Retrieved from http://www.jstor.org/stable/30140133.

Perkins, D. D., & Zimmerman, M. A. (1995). Empowerment theory, research and application. *American Journal of Community Psychology, 23*(5), 569-579. https://doi.org/10.1007/BF02506982.

Peters, R. M. (2006). The relationship of racism, chronic stress emotions and blood pressure. *Journal of Nursing Scholarship, 38*(3), 234-240. https://doi.org/10.1111/j.1547-5069.2006.00108.x.

Pew Research Center. (2016, September 13). The parties on the eve of the 2016 election: Two coalitions, moving further apart. Retrieved from https://www.pewresearch.org/politics/2016/09/13/2-party-affiliation-among-voters-1992-2016/#:~:text=Trends%20in%20party%20affiliation%20among,as%20Republican%20or%20lean%20Republican.

Pew Research Center. (2021, February 16). Faith among Black Americans. Retrieved from https://www.pewresearch.org/religion/2021/02/16/faith-among-black-americans/.

Pew Research Center. (2022, August 30). Black Americans have a clear vision for reducing racism but little hope it will happen. Retrieved from https://www.pewresearch.org/race-and-ethnicity/2022/08/30/black-americans-have-a-clear-vision-for-reducing-racism-but-little-hope-it-will-happen/.

Pieterse, A. L., Todd, N. R., Neville, H. A., & Carter, R. T. (2012). Perceived racism and mental health among Black American adults: A meta-analytic review. *Journal of Counseling Psychology, 59*(1), 1-9. https://doi.org/10.1037/a0026208.

Pitas, N., & Ehmer, C. (2020). Social capital in the response to COVID-19. *American Journal of Health Promotion, 34*(8), 942-944. https://doi.org/10.1177/0890117120924531.

Poortinga, W. (2011). Community resilience and health: The role of bonding, bridging and linking aspects of social capital. *Health & Place, 18*(2), 286-295. https://doi.org/10.1016/j.healthplace.2011.09.017.

Portes, A. (1998). Social capital: Its origins and applications in modern sociology. *Annual Review of Sociology, 24*, 1-24. Retrieved July 5, 2012, from http://digicult.net/moss_texts/SOCIALCAPITAL_ItsOriginsandApplicationsinModernSociology.pdf.

Portes, A., & Vickstrom, E. (2011). Diversity, social capital, and cohesion. *Annual Review of Sociology, 37*, 461-479. https://doi.org/10.1146/annurev-soc-081309-150022.

Price, P. L. (2010). At the crossroads: Critical race theory and critical geographies of race. *Progress in Human Geography, 34*(2), 147-174. https://doi.org/10.1177/0309132509339005.

Pulido, L. (2000). Rethinking environmental racism: White privilege and urban development in Southern California. *Annals of the Association of American Geographers, 90*(1), 12-40. https://doi.org/10.1111/0004-5608.00182.

Putnam, R. D. (1993). The prosperous community: Social capital and public life. *The American Prospect, 4*(13), 1-11. Retrieved April 16, 2012, fromhttp://prospect.org/article/prosperous-community-social-capital-and-public-life.

Putnam, R. D. (2000). *Bowling alone: The collapse and revival of American community.* Simon & Schuster.

Putnam, R. D. (2007). E pluribus unum: Diversity and community in the twenty-first century the 2006 Johan Skytte Prize Lecture. *Scandinavian Political Studies, 30*(2), 134-175. Retrieved from http://www.abdn.ac.uk/sociology/notes07/Level4/SO4530/Assigned-Readings/Reading%209%20(new).pdf.

Pyke, K. (2010). What is internalized racial oppression and why don't we study it? Acknowledging racism's hidden injuries. *Sociological Perspectives, 53*(4), 551-572. https://doi.org/10.1525/sop.2010.53.4.551.

Pyles, L., & Cross, T. (2008). Community revitalization in post-Katrina New Orleans: A critical analysis of social capital in an African American neighborhood. *Journal of Community Practice, 16*(4), 383-401. https://doi.org/10.1080/10705420802475050.

Ravanera, Z. R., & Rajulton, F. (2010). Measuring social capital and its differentials by family structures. *Social Indicators Research, 95*(1), 63-89. https://doi.org/10.1007/s11205-009-9450-9.

Rees, C. A., Monuteaux, M. C., Steidley, I., Mannix, R., Lee, L. K., Barrett, J. T., & Fleegler, E. W. (2022). Trends and disparities in firearm fatalities in the United States, 1990-2021. *JAMA Network Open, 5*(11), e2244221.https://doi.org/10.1001/jamanetworkopen.2022.44221.

Renya, C. P., Korfmacher, W., & Tucker, A. (2005). Examining the principles in principled conservatism: The role of responsibility stereotypes as cues for deservingness in racial policy decisions. *Journal of Personality and Social Psychology, 90*(1), 109-128. https://doi.org/10.1037/0022-3514.90.1.109.

Roberts, D. E. (2004). The social and moral cost of mass incarceration in African American communities. *Stanford Law Review, 56*(5), 1271-1304. Retrieved from https://www.law.upenn.edu/cf/faculty/roberts1/workingpapers/b56StanLRev1271(2004).pdf.

Roque, A. D., Pijawka, D., & Wutich, A. (2020). The role of social capital in resiliency: Disaster recovery in Puerto Rico. *Risk, Hazards, and Crisis in Public Policy, 11*(2), 204-235. https://doi.org/10.1002/rhc3.12197.

Rose, D., & Clear, T. (2003). Incarceration, reentry, and social capital: Social networks in the balance. In J. Travis, & M. Waul (Eds.), *Prisoners once removed: The impact of incarceration and reentry on children, families, and communities* (pp. 313-342). The Urban Institute Press.

Salvatore, S. C., Garcia, M., Hornsby, A., Lawson, S., & Mah, T. (2009). *Civil rights in America: Racial desegregation of public accommodations.* The National Historic Landmarks Program.

Selman, P. (2010). Social capital, sustainability and environmental planning. *Planning Theory & Practice, 2*(1), 13-30. https://doi.org/10.1080/14649350020008396.

Shofner, J. H. (1977). Custom, law and history: The enduring influence of Florida's Black code. *The Florida Historical Quarterly, 55*(3), 277-298. Retrieved from http://www.jstor.org/stable/30149151.

Solorzano, D., Ceja, M., & Yosso, T. (2000). Critical race theory, racial microaggressions and campus climate: The experiences of African American college students. *The Journal of Negro Education, 69*(1/2), 60-73. Retrieved from http://www.ryanbowenphoto.com/home/blog/Entries/2006/12/31_Black_men_files/racial%20microaggressions.pdf.

Son Hing, L. S., Hamilton, L. K., & Zanna, M. P. (2008). A two-dimensional model that employs explicit and implicit attitudes to characterize prejudice. *Journal of Personality and Social Psychology, 94*(6), 971-987. https://doi.org/10.1037/0022-3514.94.6.971.

Sonn, C. C., & Quayle, A. F. (2013). Developing praxis: Mobilizing critical race theory in community cultural development. *Journal of Community & Applied Social Psychology, 23*(5), 435-448. https://doi.org/10.1002/casp.2145.

Spaans, M., & Waterhout, B. (2017). Building up resilience in cities worldwide—Rotterdam as participant in the 100 resilient cities programme. *Cities, 61*, 109-116. https://doi.org/10.1016/j.cities.2016.05.011.

Spatig-Amerikaner, A. (2012). Unequal education: Federal loophole allows lower spending on students of color. *Center for American Progress.* Retrieved from www.americanprogress.org.

Speight, S. L. (2007). Internalized racism: One more piece of the puzzle. *The Counseling Psychologist, 35*(1), 126-134. https://doi.org/10.1177/0011000006295119.

Steinfield, C., DiMicco, J., Ellison, N. B., & Lampe, C. (2009). Bowling online: Social networking and social capital within the organization. *Proceedings of the Fourth International Conference on Communities and Technologies* (pp. 245-254). ACM. https://doi.org/10.1145/1556460.1556496.

Stovall, D. (2012). Against the politics of desperation: Educational justice, critical race theory, and Chicago school reform. *Critical Studies in Education, 54*(1), 33-43. https://doi.org/10.1080/17508487.2013.739192.

Strayhorn, T. L. (2010). When race and gender collide: Social and cultural capital's influence on the academic achievement of African American and Latino males. *The Review of Higher Education, 33*(3), 307-332. Retrieved from http://smtpgw.qem.org/QEM2010Workshops/MINORITY_MALES_INITI-ATIVE/AAMalesPresentations/33.3.strayhorn.pdf.

Strouble, B. W. Jr. (2015). Racism vs. social capital: A case study of two majority Black communities. *Scholar Works.*

Sue, D. W. (2003). *Overcoming our racism: The journey to liberation.* Jossey-Bass.

Sue, D. W., Capodilupo, C. M., Torino, G. C., Bucceri, J. M., Holder, A. M., Nadal, K. L., & Esquilin, M. (2007). Racial microaggressions in everyday life: Implications for clinical practice. *American Psychologist, 62*(4), 271-286. https://doi.org/10.1037/0003-066X.62.4.271.

Sullivan, J. (2011). African Americans moving south and to the suburbs. *Race, Poverty, and the Environment, 18*(2), 16-19.

Tatum, B. (2007). Defining racism. In M. L. Andersen & P. H. Collins (Eds.), *Race, class, and gender in the United States: An integrated study* (pp. 123-128). Wadsworth.

Teilmann, K. (2012). Measuring social capital accumulation in rural development. *Journal of Rural Studies, 28*(4), 458-465. https://doi.org/10.1016/j.jrurstud.2012.10.002.

Tesler, M. (2013). The return to old-fashioned racism to White Americans' partisan preferences in the early Obama era. *The Journal of Politics, 75*(1), 110-123. https://doi.org/10.1017/S00223381620009042.

Torres, A. P., Marshall, M. I., & Sydnor, S. (2019). Does social capital pay off? The case of small business resilience after Hurricane Katrina. *Journal of Contingencies and Crisis Management, 27*(2), 168-181. https://doi.org/10.1111/1468-5973.12248.

U.S Census Bureau. (2015b). 2009-2013 5-Year American Community Survey, Leon County. Retrieved March 30, 2015, from American Fact Finder:http://factfinder.census.gov/.

U.S. Census Bureau. (2022). American Community Survey (ACS). Retrieved December 30, 2023, from https://data.census.gov/table/ACSDT5Y2022.B02001?q=B02001:%20RACE&t=Race%20and%20Ethnicity&g=010XX00US$1400000.

U.S. Department of Education. (2023). Table 302.20. Percentage of recent high school completers enrolled in college, by race/ethnicity and level of institution: 1960 through 2022. Retrieved from https://nces.ed.gov/programs/digest/d23/tables/dt23_302.20.asp.

Uggen, C., Shannon, S., & Manza, J. (2012). State-Level estimates of felon disenfranchisement in the United States, 2010. The Sentencing Project. Washington D.C: The Sentencing Project.

Urquidez, A. G. (2020). *(Re-) defining racism: A philosophical analysis.* Springer Nature.

Vaught, S. E., & Castagno, A. E. (2008). "I don't think I'm a racist": Critical race theory, teacher attitudes and structural racism. *Race Ethnicity and Education, 11*(2), 95-113. https://doi.org/10.1080/13613320802110217.

Verhaeghe, P.-P., Pattyn, E., Bracke, P., Verhaeghe, M., & Van De Putte, B. (2011). The association between network social capital and self-rated health: Pouring old wine in new bottles? *Health & Place, 17*(1), 358-365. https://doi.org/10.1016/j.healthplace.2010.11.001.

Violence Policy Center. (2023). Black homicide victimization in the United States: An analysis of 2020 homicide data. Retrieved fromhttps://vpc.org/black-homicide-victimization-in-the-united-states/.

Wakefield, S. E., & Baxter, J. (2010). Linking health inequality and environmental justice: Articulating a precautionary framework for research and action. *Environmental Justice, 3*(3), 95-102. https://doi.org/10.1089/env.2009.0044.

Walsh, J. (2012). Swept under the rug: Integrating critical race theory into the legal debate on the use of race. *Seattle Journal for Social Justice, 6*(2), 673-726. Retrieved fromhttp://digitalcommons.law.seattleu.edu/sjsj/vol6/iss2/13.

Welle, T., Witting, M., Birkman, J., & Brossmann, M. (2014). Assessing and monitoring climate resilience: From theoretical considerations to practically applicable tools. *Federal Ministry for Economic Cooperation and Development (BMZ) Special Unit 'Climate'. Berlin: Deutsche Gesellschaft für Internationale Zusammenarbeit (GIZ).

Wilcox, B., Wang, W., & Rowe, I. (2021). Less poverty, less prison, more college: What two parents mean for Black and White children. *Institute for Family Studies.*

Wilson, S. M., Richard, R., Lesley, J., & Williams, E. (2010). Climate change, environmental justice and vulnerability: An exploratory spatial analysis. *Environmental Justice, 3*(1), 13-18. https://doi.org/10.1089/env.2009.0033.

Wilson, W. J. (2011). The declining significance of race: Revisited and revised. *Daedalus, 140*(2), 55-69. https://doi.org/10.1162/DAED_a_00077.

Woolley, M. E., Grogan-Kaylor, A., Gilster, M. E., Karb, R. A., Grant, L. M., Reischl, T. M., & Alaimo, K. (2008). Neighborhood social capital, poor physical conditions and school achievement. *Children and Schools, 30*(3), 133-145. https://doi.org/10.1093/cs/30.3.133.

Wright, R., Ellis, M., Holloway, S., & Wong, S. (2013). Patterns of racial diversity and segregation in the United States 1990-2010. *The Professional Geographer, 65*(4), 613-625. https://doi.org/10.1080/00330124.2012.735924.

Yang, S., Keller, F. B., & Zheng, L. (2017). *Social network analysis: Methods and examples.* Sage.

Yin, R. K. (2009). *Case study research: Design and methods.* Sage.

Yosso, T. J., Smith, W. A., Ceja, M., & Solorzano, D. G. (2009). Critical race theory, racial microaggressions, and campus racial climate for Latina/o undergraduates.

Harvard Educational Review, 79(4), 659-690. Retrieved fromhttp://her.hepg.org/content/m6867014157m707l/.

Zurita, M. D., Cook, B., Thomsen, D., Munro, P. G., Smith, T. F., & Gallina, J. (2018). Living with disasters: Social capital for disaster governance. *Disasters, 42*(3), 571-589. https://doi.org/10.1111/disa.12257.

About the Author

Dr. Bruce W. Strouble is an esteemed anti-racism scholar, environmental justice advocate, and community organizer rooted in Pasadena, California, currently residing in Tallahassee, Florida. With a deep commitment to advancing sustainability and resilience in African American communities, Dr. Strouble holds a Ph.D. in Public Policy and Administration from Walden University, complemented by African American Studies and Social Sciences studies at Florida A&M University.

Dr. Strouble's career spans impactful roles, including Sustainability Program Coordinator for the City of Tallahassee and Sustainability Coordinator at Florida A&M University's Sustainability Institute. He is the Senior Manager of Equitable Climate Resilience Programs at Groundwork USA, leading initiatives that empower communities to confront climate challenges through democratic engagement and equitable solutions.

Recognized for his leadership, Dr. Strouble received the 2018 ReThink Energy Florida "Energy Innovator" award, a testament to his innovative approach and expertise in the field. He is a Senior Fellow at the Institute for the Polarities of Democracy and the Environmental Leadership Program. He is a founding member of Citizens for a Sustainable Future Inc. and vice President of the New Era Impact Investment Fund. He serves on the boards of the Capital City Chamber of Commerce, Rethink Energy Florida, and the Moving Forward Network.

As a father of four Black boys, Dr. Strouble's personal and professional dedication converges on fostering sustainable and cohesive communities. His influence extends through academia, where he occasionally teaches courses in Political Science, Public Policy, and African American History. Driven by a profound belief in the power of community and democracy, Dr. Strouble continues to shape policies and practices that promote environmental justice and enhance political participation across diverse landscapes, inspiring hope for a better future.